101 Fresh & Fun Critical-Thinking Activities

Engaging Activities and Reproducibles to Develop Kids' Higher-Level Thinking Skills

by Laurie Rozakis, Ph.D

S C H O L A S T I C
PROFESSIONAL BOOKS

New York ★ Toronto ★ London ★ Auckland ★ Sydney

Dedication

With love and thanks, I dedicate this book to all the fine teachers who have enriched my life: Barbara Bengels, Chris LaRosa, Ed Leigh, Jack McGrath, Jim Pepperman, Jennifer Richmond, Elizabeth Simmons, Lenore Strober, and Tom Thibadeau.

Scholastic Inc. grants teachers permission to photocopy the activity sheets from this book for classroom use. No other part of this publication may be reproduced in whole or in part, or stored in a retrieval system, or transmitted in any form or by any means, without written permission of the publisher. For information regarding permission, write to Scholastic Professional Books, 555 Broadway, New York, NY 10012-3999.

Cover design and illustration by Jaime Lucero
Interior design by Jaime Lucero and Robert Dominguez for Grafica, Inc.
Interior illustrations by Maxie Chambliss and Mary Lou Cramer

ISBN: 0-590-37523-7

Contents

Introduction

What is critical thinking? It's the ability to:

- **solve problems**
- **make products that are valued in a particular culture.**
- **locate the appropriate route to a goal.**
- **capture and transmit knowledge.**
- **express one's views and feelings appropriately.**

Effective critical thinkers use one or more of the seven multiple intelligences identified by Dr. Howard Gardner:

1. **verbal/linguistic intelligence**
2. **logical/mathematical intelligence**
3. **visual/spatial intelligence**
4. **bodily/kinesthetic intelligence**
5. **musical/rhythmic intelligence**
6. **interpersonal intelligence (work cooperatively in a group)**
7. **intrapersonal intelligence (self-identity)**

Research indicates that critical thinking is neither inborn nor naturally acquired. In fact, fewer than half the adults in America today have the ability to reflect upon their thinking and explain how they solved a problem.

The good news? Critical thinking *can* be taught and learned. This book, and its companion volume for grades 4-6, is designed to help you teach children to reflect upon their own thinking processes, and in so doing, become more successful, active learners. Both professional educators and parents can use this book to help children learn to think critically.

In our daily lives we use many critical-thinking skills simultaneously—and not in any prescribed order. In this book, however, the activities are arranged in a hierarchy—from easiest to more difficult—so that you and your students can more clearly understand and identify the specific critical thinking skills involved.

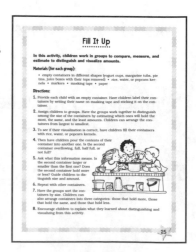

For each thinking skill in the book, there are two kinds of activities: 1) those that you, as the teacher, will lead (shown at right), and 2) student reproducibles for independent work (shown on the following page). On the

Teacher Page

4

introductory pages for each section of the book, you'll find ideas for introducing and using the student reproducibles. You can use the Try This! activity at the bottom of each reproducible as an extension of the lesson, a challenge activity, or a homework assignment.

Student Page

Here are some ways you can use the lessons to help children become more effective thinkers:

1. Read each activity aloud or have a child read it aloud to the rest of the group.
2. Allow children ample time to think and respond.
3. Ask students questions to assess their understanding of the problem.
4. Welcome different strategies for solving the problem. Encourage divergent thinking.
5. Observe children as they work in order monitor their problem-solving skills.
6. Give helpful hints to those children who are having difficulty finding ways to approach the problem.
7. Guide children to link the problem to others they have already solved.
8. Encourage children to check their work.
9. Help children explore their thinking and identify the strategies that worked—and those that didn't.
10. Invite students to share their results.

Since critical thinking doesn't end when an individual project does, you will want to give children sufficient time to evaluate their thinking strategies. Guide children to formulate ways they might adjust their critical-thinking strategies with the next problems they solve.

Finally, model critical thinking for your students by sharing your own problem-solving strategies and accepting unusual and unexpected strategies and solutions. Your participation as an active learner will further reinforce the critical-thinking skills you teach.

Above all, encourage your students to see themselves as thinkers.

Recognizing and Recalling Activities

To begin thinking critically, children must first learn to recognize and recall key information. These skills are important for the mastery of higher-level skills such as classification, inferring, and analyzing.

The activities in this section will help students tap their prior knowledge to identify and remember key facts. You can present each activity as a complete lesson or integrate the activities into lessons in different curriculum areas. The section begins with the easier activities and concludes with more difficult ones. Instructions for teacher-led activities appear on the same page as the activity. Use the teacher notes that follow for the student reproducibles.

Cross-Curricular Links

Teacher Notes for Student Reproducibles

Page 9: What I Can Do

In this activity students recall their own accomplishments. For younger children, you may wish to have them draw pictures or tell the class orally about the things they can do. For older students, you might use the Try This! as a portfolio piece. Have students reread their paragraph later in the school year to note any progress.

Page 11: Newspaper Hunt

A newspaper treasure hunt is an effective way to teach children how to recognize and recall information. It is also a good way to introduce children to the newspaper as a source of information. Divide the class into teams or small groups and distribute a newspaper to each group. Duplicate the reproducible on page 11 and give a copy to each group. Instruct students to go on a "treasure hunt" to find the items on the chart. Depending on students' level, you can ask that they find pictures or words or both. Have students circle the item on the chart and write the section and page number below.

Pages 14–15: Place the Pictures, I and II

These pages ask that children recall and identify items that are appropriate for different places. If children circle a picture that is not usually found in the designated place, encourage them to explain why they circled it. Accept any reasonable or creative explanations. For example, a child might say that a supermarket had a cut-out figure of a gorilla as part of a display.

Pages 16–17: Animals, Animals, I and II

The first of these pages focuses on size comparisons, while the second requires children to identify other attributes of animals. As students recall animals for each category, you may suggest that they draw additional animals on another sheet of paper. Older students may draw just one animal and write the names of others. Follow-up by compiling a class list of all the animals students drew for each category.

Page 18: A Is for . . .

Set aside time for students to compare and discuss their finished lists. Although this activity calls for writing, you can adapt it for younger children by compiling a class list on the chalkboard. Be sure children understand the difference between growing and nongrowing things beforehand.

Page 19: Who Lives Here?

As students share their finished pictures, encourage them to tell how they knew which animals to draw. Discuss different ways that we get information.

Page 20: Fruit Salad Chart

Explain that a chart is a way of organizing information so it is easier to read. As children fill in the chart, point out that they can read it by looking across and down.

Page 21: Word Meaning Fun

Before passing out this page, you may wish to introduce the term *homonym* (words with the same sound and often the same spelling, but different meanings).

I Like You

This is a great activity to use in September, but it is equally effective at any time during the year.

With the class, share Arnold Lobel's *Frog and Toad Are Friends* (Harper-Collins) or another grade-appropriate book that talks about friends and friendship. Then ask children to complete this sentence:

A friend is _____ .

List students' ideas on the chalkboard and discuss the various ways friends show they care. Encourage students to recall specific ways friends have acted toward them. Children might suggest that friends help each other by sharing food or belongings, by helping one another, or by talking about feelings.

Ask children to form a "friendship circle" by sitting in a circle and linking hands. Join the circle yourself. One at a time, have children turn to the person next to them and say something positive about them, such as "I like the way you share the crayons" or "I like the way you sing" or "I like it when you wait for me on the playground."

To complete the lesson, teach children the lyrics to this traditional friendship rhyme and discuss its meaning: "Make new friends, but keep the old; one is silver and the other gold."

What I Can Do

Think of the things you have learned to do by yourself. What a long list! Now fill in the blank to complete each sentence.

> I can do many things on my own.

On my own, I can _____.

On my own, I can _____.

On my own, I can _____.

On my own, I can _____.

On my own, I can _____.

On my own, I can _____.

 **Try This!** **Write Your Thoughts** Choose one thing you wrote about that is still hard for you to do by yourself. Write a paragraph explaining why.

Name That Coin

Children love to look at coins but sometimes they have difficulty recognizing and recalling their value. This activity will help students familiarize themselves with coins. You might integrate the activity into a math lesson on money. You can work with small groups or the whole class.

Materials:

quarters   dimes
nickels   pennies

Directions:

1. Distribute the coins and invite volunteers to provide the following information:
  - the color of the coin
  - the pictures on the front and back of each coin
  - what each coin is worth

2. Let children handle the coins and learn to recognize them.

3. Then place a penny, nickel, and dime on a table.

4. Tell children you are thinking of one of these coins, but don't name it. Instead, give hints to help children recognize the coin you have in mind. For example, you can say, "My coin has a man on one side and a building on the other."

5. Invite children to make guesses. Provide other clues as needed, such as, "My coin is silver."

6. Play several rounds of the game. After some time, you may want to introduce the quarter as well.

7. After everyone has guessed at least one coin correctly, discuss other ways to recognize coins.

Newspaper Hunt

box

section _____
page _____

food

section _____
page _____

building

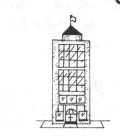

section _____
page _____

sport

section _____
page _____

car

section _____
page _____

dog

section _____
page _____

woman

section _____
page _____

map

section _____
page _____

truck

section _____
page _____

 **Try This!**

Tell a Story Make up a story about one of the pictures you found. Tell it to the class.

Quick Change Game

This game is a favorite with students, and you can play it at different levels of difficulty. To begin, sit the entire class in a circle, making sure that everyone has a clear view of the center.

Explain that this game will test students' ability to remember what someone looks like and to recognize any changes in his or her appearance.

Next, ask two volunteers to stand in the center of the circle. Give them ten to twenty seconds to study each other closely. Then have them turn their backs to one another and change three things about their appearance. Begin with obvious changes such as taking off a pair of glasses or removing a sneaker. Then move to more subtle changes such as removing a barrette or untying a shoe. Once the changes are made, have the volunteers turn around to face each other. Give them ten to twenty seconds to find all the changes. When their time is up, have the volunteers state whether their partner's observations were correct. Continue the game, using new pairs of volunteers, until everyone in the class has had a chance in the center of the circle.

As the game progresses, you can reduce the observation time, increase the number of changes, and suggest that children make their changes more subtle.

Story Details

Here is a literature-based activity to help students develop their recognition and recalling skills.

Select a story that children have read or that you have read to them. You may want to reread the story with the class before you begin to make sure that everyone is familiar with it.

Explain that you are going to list details from the story on the chalkboard. Some of the details will really come from the story; others will not. Ask children to identify which details come from the story. Here's a sample list from Syd Hoff's *Danny and the Dinosaur* (Harper and Row):

> **Danny went to the museum. (*from the story*)**
>
> **He went with his parents. (*not from the story*)**
>
> **He saw dinosaurs. (*from the story*)**
>
> **A dinosaur took Danny for a ride. (*from the story*)**
>
> **They saw other dinosaurs on the street. (*not from the story*)**
>
> **Danny and the dinosaur visited the zoo. (*from the story*)**

Next, ask children to add two more details that come from the story. For example, for *Danny and the Dinosaur* they might add that Danny gave other children a ride on the dinosaur, Danny learned tricks, or Danny played hide-and-seek.

Continue this activity by having children work in pairs or small groups to make up a list of details from another story the class has read, adding two or three details that they have "invented." Have each team present its list to the class. Encourage other students to distinguish between details that come from the story and details that do not.

Place the Pictures, I

Circle the things you find at a beach.

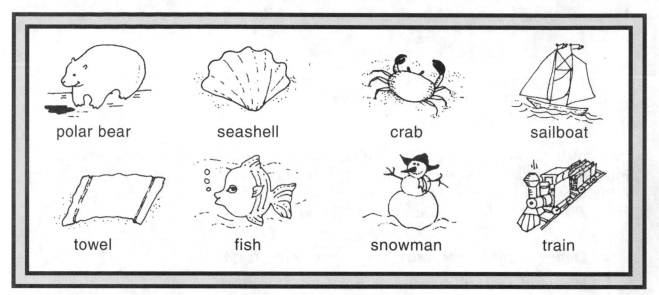

polar bear   seashell   crab   sailboat

towel   fish   snowman   train

Circle the things you find at a supermarket.

shopping cart   pond   horse   magazine

bread   bananas   milk   campfire

 **Try This!**

Add More Think of two more things you might find at the beach. Think of two more things you might find at the supermarket.

Name _____

Place the Pictures, II

Circle the things you find at a zoo.

tree   toothbrush   monkey   elephant

tiger   bear   dinosaur   violin

Circle the things you find in school.

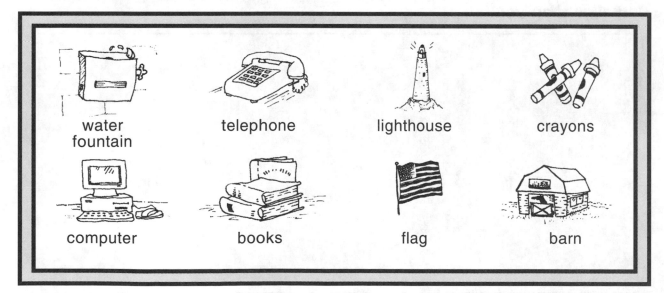

water fountain   telephone   lighthouse   crayons

computer   books   flag   barn

 **Try This!**

In the Classroom Draw 6 things you would find in the classroom. Draw 3 things that you would not find in the classroom. Have a friend play your game.

15

Animals, Animals, I

In the space below, draw as many animals as you can that are bigger than you.

In the space below, draw as many animals as you can that are smaller than you.

 Try This! **Share and Compare** Compare your pictures with a classmate's. How many of the same animals did you draw? How many different animals did you draw?

Animals, Animals, II

In the space below, draw as many animals as you can that have fur.

In the space below, draw as many animals as you can that are green.

 **Try This!**   **Find More**   Use a book to find more animals that you can add to this page.

Name _____

A Is for . . .
· · · · · · · · · · · · · · · ·

So many things grow! Make this ABC list grow. Write the name of something that grows and begins with each letter. It might be a fruit, vegetable, tree, flower, or an animal. The first one is done for you.

A is for ___Apple___ .   N is for _____.

B is for _____ .   O is for _____.

C is for _____ .   P is for _____.

D is for _____ .   Q is for _____.

E is for _____ .   R is for _____.

F is for _____ .   S is for _____.

G is for _____ .   T is for _____.

H is for _____ .   U is for _____.

I is for _____ .   V is for _____.

J is for _____ .   W or X is for _____.

K is for _____ .   Y is for _____.

L is for _____ .   Z is for _____.

M is for _____ .

 **Try This!**   **Another List** Make a new ABC list for things that move. For each letter, write one thing that moves.

18

Who Lives Here?

Animals live in different kinds of homes. Draw a picture of an animal that might live in each of these homes.

barn

hive

lake

nest

tree

cave

Try This!

Another Home

Draw a picture of *your* home! Draw yourself inside.

Fruit Salad Chart

A chart is used to show information. A chart can show many different kinds of information.

Read this chart.
1. Read the words at the left.
2. Read the words at the top.
3. Put an X if the word tells about the fruit.
4. Put a 0 if it does not.

FRUITS	red	yellow	purple	orange	round
1. orange					
2. banana					
3. lemon					
4. grapes					
5. pineapple					

Try This! **Recall More**   On another sheet of paper, draw 3 green vegetables, 2 yellow vegetables, and 1 orange vegetable. Write the name of each vegetable.

Word Meaning Fun

You use some words in more than one way.

head   or   head

eye   or   eye

elbows	neck
heel	toe
body	skin
ear	face
teeth	eye
hands	

The words in the grey box above are all parts of your body. You use these words to describe parts of other things, too. Write a word or words from the box that are also parts of the items below. You can use a word more than once.

1. clock _____

2. potato _____

3. zipper _____

4. socks _____

5. corn _____

6. saw _____

7. macaroni _____

8. shirt _____

9. car _____

10. storm _____

 Try This! **Word Search** Find things with these body parts: mouth, neck, tongue, arms, and legs. Draw pictures of them on another sheet of paper.

Distinguishing and Visualizing Activities

When children become skilled at distinguishing between important and unimportant data and visualizing problem-solving strategies, they naturally develop more logical and effective patterns of thinking. The activities in this section will help students learn to identify specific items and form strong mental images.

Use the chart to help you relate the activities in this section to your class curriculum. In general, the easier activities appear at the beginning of the section, and the more difficult ones follow. Instructions for teacher-led activities are on the same page as the activity. Notes for using the student reproducibles follow the chart.

Cross-Curricular Links

Activity	Page	Content Area
Where Do You Wear It?	24	science/social studies
Fill It Up	25	mathematics/science
Alphabet Soup	26	language arts
Number Fun	27	mathematics
Match the Mice	28	mathematics
Some Are the Same	29	science/mathematics
Words and Pictures	30	language arts
Using Your Senses	31	art/science
Fun with Words	32	art/language arts
What Does It Look Like?	33	art/language arts
Naming Sets	34	mathematics/language arts
Card Games	35	mathematics
Definitions and Examples	36	language arts
Mixed-Up Words	37	language arts
Syllable Count	38-39	language arts/mathematics

Teacher Notes for Student Reproducibles

Page 24: Where Do You Wear It?
This activity calls for students to distinguish among various items of clothing and accessories to visualize where they are worn. In addition to writing the correct part of the body, you may also have students color the items according to a code—for example: blue for hands, brown for feet, red for head, and yellow for body.

Page 27: Number Fun
This activity for younger children focuses on number correspondence. Ask children to explain how they knew which bone each dog got.

Page 28: Match the Mice
This activity is similar to the one on page 27 but involves cutting and pasting. Be sure to pass out scissors and glue along with the page.

Page 29: Some Are the Same
As students identify similarities and differences in the pictures, ask them to describe ways that the pictures are alike and different.

Page 30: Words and Pictures
On this page, students work with definitions and examples. Once children complete the page, have them share the various pictures they drew.

Page 31: Using Your Senses
Before passing out this page, review the five senses of seeing, hearing, tasting, touching, and smelling. After students draw their pictures, ask them to tell which senses are involved with each thing.

Page 32: Fun with Words
The word pictures on this page are sometimes called "wordles." You may wish to discuss the meaning of each word before students complete the page. Be sure to invite children to share their finished word pictures.

Page 33: What Does It Look Like?
This activity calls for students to exercise their imaginations. You may wish to model thinking for the first word beforehand. For example: "Clodpod makes me think of dirt and beans. I think a clodpod is a kind of vegetable so I'll draw it like this . . ." Consider making a class book that shows all the different pictures for each word.

Page 34: Naming Sets
The skills used in this activity are important for the mastery of classification. The activity also provides practice in observation. Discuss the examples before students complete the page.

Page 36: Definitions and Examples
This page requires students to use illustrations to differentiate among three possible words for each definition. Encourage students to verbalize their thinking in a follow-up discussion.

Page 37: Mixed-Up Words
In this activity, students visualize simple words for kitchen items. For younger students, you may wish to list the words on the chalkboard so that after they identify a picture, children can check the word's spelling.

Where Do You Wear It?

Write the word that tells where you wear each thing.

head	feet	hands	body

1.
_____

2.
_____

3.
_____

4.
_____

5.
_____

6.
_____

7.
_____

8.
_____

9.
_____

10.
_____

11.
_____

12.
_____

 Try This!

One More Think of one more thing to wear on each part of your body.

Fill It Up

In this activity, children work in groups to compare, measure, and estimate to distinguish and visualize amounts.

Materials (for each group):

- empty containers in different shapes (yogurt cups, margarine tubs, pie tins, juice boxes with tops removed) • rice, water, or popcorn kernels • markers • masking tape • paper

Directions:

1. Provide each child with an empty container. Have children label their containers by writing their name on masking tape and sticking it on the container.

2. Assign children to groups. Have the groups work together to distinguish among the size of the containers by estimating which ones will hold the most, the same, and the least amounts. Children can arrange the containers from largest to smallest.

3. To see if their visualization is correct, have children fill their containers with rice, water, or popcorn kernels.

4. Then have children pour the contents of their container into another one. Is the second container overflowing, full, half full, or not full?

5. Ask what this information means. Is the second container larger or smaller than the first one? Does the second container hold more or less? Guide children to distinguish size and amount.

6. Repeat with other containers.

7. Have the groups sort the containers by size. Children can also arrange containers into three categories: those that hold more, those that hold the same, and those that hold less.

8. Encourage children to explain what they learned about distinguishing and visualizing from this activity.

Alphabet Soup

Here's an activity that's both educational and delicious!

Materials:

- breakfast cereal or pasta letters
- paper and pencils
- glue

Directions:

1. Before class, sort through the letters to pick out those suitable for forming simple words. For beginning readers, for example, select letters such as C, A, T, D, O, and G. For more advanced readers, select letters needed to form more complex words. For an extra challenge, you may wish to have children pick out a handful of letters at random. Regardless of grade level, make sure everyone has enough letters to form words they know.

2. Ask students to work individually or in pairs to form as many words as they can from the letters. For beginning readers, allow at least five minutes for each round; allow less time for more advanced readers. Explain that students do not have to use all the letters for each word, and that words can have as few as one letter. No fair biting off parts of an E to make an F! Ask children to write down each word as they form it, since the letters may move around.

3. When time is up, have volunteers list their letters and the words they formed on the board. Then invite the rest of the class to look at the words on the board and contribute any additional ones they made.

4. At the end of the activity, children can eat the cereal letters and glue their pasta words onto a sheet of paper.

Number Fun

1. Count the spots on each dog.
2. Look at the numbers on the bones.
3. Draw a line from each dog to its bone.

**Try This!**

More Dogs   Draw a dog with 7 spots. Write the number on his bone.

Match the Mice

1. Count the holes in each slice of cheese.
2. Count the mice in each circle.
3. Cut out the circles of mice.
4. Paste each circle of mice to the dotted circle on the right slice of cheese with the same number of holes as mice.

Try This!

Count How many mice are there in all?

Some Are the Same

1. Color two animals that are the same.
2. Circle the third animal that is not the same.

1.

2.

3.

4.

5.

 **Try This!**

Change the Picture
Make all the rabbits
the same.

Words and Pictures

1. Read the word in each box.
2. Draw a picture to show what the word means.
3. Write one of these sentences under the picture it tells about.

    This is something you play with.

    This is something you sleep on.

    This is something you eat.

    This is something to wear on your head.

food	hat

bed	toy

 **Try This!**   **Compare Pictures** Look at the pictures that a friend made. How are they like yours? How are they different?

Using Your Senses

Draw these things:

a sticky thing	**a sour thing**
a hot thing	**a noisy thing**
a spicy thing	**a wet thing**

Try This! **More About the Senses** On another sheet of paper, draw the parts of your body you use for seeing, smelling, tasting, and hearing.

31

Name _____

Fun with Words

You can make some words look like their meaning.
Look at the word wide.
The letters are wide.

Write or draw each of these words so as to show what they mean.

1. tall	2. shake
3. crack	4. thin
5. fat	6. round

 **Try This!**   **More Words** Think of another word that you could write or draw so as to show its meaning.

What Does It Look Like?

Cat, apple, and boat are real words. You can make up words, too!
Here are some made-up words. What do they mean? Draw a picture
to show what you think.

clodpod	**banlam**
tedfus	**zeddie**
panci	**geedee**

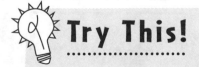 **Try This!** **Make up More** Make up five words of your own.
Draw a picture for each one.

Naming Sets

A set is a collection of things. The things can be people, numbers, or anything else! The members of the set are like each other in one or more ways. Here are two sets. How are the members alike?

All the members of the set are cats.

All the members of the set are numbers.

Look at the things in each set. Write one way that they are the same.

1.

_____

_____

2.

_____

_____

3.

_____

_____

4.

_____

_____

 **Try This!**

Make a Set Draw a set of things that you would find at the park.

Card Games
. . . .

These games help children learn to distinguish between numbers and to draw sharp mental images.

Make 100

Materials (for pair of students):

> playing cards [1 (ace) - 6 in every suit]
> paper
> pencil or pen

Directions:

1. Explain that the object of the game is to make a sum as close to 100 as possible—but not over! Each player decides whether to use a card in the tens place or the ones place.

2. Pair children and have each player draw 8 cards from the pack.

3. Model how to play. For example, if a player draws two 1s (aces), a 2, a 5, two 3s, a 4, and a 6, the player can use the numerals in the following way: 30, 40, 10, 5, 6, 1, 3, 2 = 97. Point out which cards were used in the tens place (3, 4, 1) and which in the ones place (5, 6, 1, 3, 2).

Bigger and Bigger

Materials (for pair of students):

> playing cards [1 (ace) - 9 in every suit]
> paper
> pencil or pen

Directions:

1. Explain that the object of this game is to make the largest 4-digit number possible.
2. To play, partners take turns drawing one card at a time.
3. Continue until each player has 5 cards. At that point, each player chooses one card to throw out and tries to make the largest possible 4-digit number.

Name _____

Definitions and Examples

Read each definition and its examples.
Circle the word that names the example in the picture.

1.

an animal with feathers

robin
duck
swan

2.

something you can sit on

stool
high chair
armchair

3.

a tool for writing

pen
pencil
crayon

4.

a green vegetable

peas
beans
lettuce

5.

something to read

newspaper
book
letter

6.

a way to tell time

clock
watch
sundial

 Try This!

Define It Choose something in the classroom. Write a definition for it.

Mixed-Up Words

The pictures show things that you would find in a kitchen.
Think of the word for each picture.
Then unscramble the letters below to form the words you thought of.

1. puc _____

2. sslag _____

3. okrf _____

4. inks _____

5. rja _____

6. shdi _____

7. otp _____

8. noosp _____

 **Try This!** **Make a List** Think of 5 more things you might find in a kitchen.

37

Syllable Count

This activity helps students learn to distinguish aural as well as visual clues by challenging them to discover the number of syllables in each of the words on page 39.

Start by selecting a word and inviting children to share the strategies they use to determine the number of syllables. Encourage them to visualize the word and tap out the number of syllables.

There are several ways you can use this activity.

Team Activity

1. Cut out each word and place the words in a bag.
2. Divide the class into two teams. Have the teams line up on opposite sides of the room.
3. Select one word at a time and ask the first player on Team A to visualize the word and identify the number of syllables it contains. If the player correctly identifies the number of syllables, give the team 1 point.
4. Select another word and call on the first player on Team B.
5. If a player cannot correctly identify the number of syllables in a word, ask a player on the other team. Alternate sides until a player correctly identifies the number of syllables.
6. The team with the most points when all the words have been called wins.

Partner Activity

1. Partners can take turns selecting slips of paper, reading the word, and identifying the number of syllables.
2. The player with the highest score wins.

Individual Activity

1. Cut out the words and write the number of syllables on the back of each word.
2. Students can try to identify the number of syllables and then check their answers by looking at the back of the paper.

Syllable Count (cont'd)

sunshine	eat	winter	Dakota
bed	bedtime	room	dangerous
beautiful	butter	day	grass
foot	lumberyard	any	after
united	grasshopper	sun	Tennessee
letter	cat	circus	animal

Activities for Following Directions and Classifying Information

After children feel comfortable distinguishing and visualizing different aspects of a problem, it is time for them to work on following directions and classifying information. The ability to follow directions helps children work through a process one step at a time. Knowing how to classify information helps them to bring order to a problem by organizing its pieces into groups based on common features.

Consider presenting one or more of the activities in this section at the start of class every day to alert children to the importance of following directions with regard to *all* their work. You'll find instructions for teacher-led activities on the same page as the activity. Notes for the student reproducibles follow the chart on this page. As in the other sections of the book, the easier activities appear first.

As children complete the activities, encourage them to think aloud. This will help you observe the thought processes that each child is using. Use the chart to help you coordinate the activities with other parts of your curriculum.

Cross-Curricular Links

Activity	Page	Content Area
A Sorting Game	42	language arts
Does It Belong?	43	language arts
Letter Code	44	language arts
Which Book?	45	language arts/social studies
Making Groups	46	language arts
Walk This Way	47	social studies
A Town Map	48	social studies
Super Sums	49	mathematics
Color by Code	50	mathematics/art
What Is What?	51	science
Riddle Me This	52	language arts
Read First!	53	language arts

Teacher Notes for Student Reproducibles

Page 42: A Sorting Game
Ask children to explain how they decided to classify each picture. Discuss additional possibilities for each group.

Page 43: Does It Belong?
You may read aloud the items in each box and have students circle the answers. Discuss students' responses.

Page 44: Letter Code
Stress that it is important to follow the directions carefully on this page. For younger children, you may want to mention that they will not change all of the letters. Have children go back and check their work if they do not solve the riddle correctly the first time.

Page 45: Which Book?
This classification activity provides an opportunity to discuss nonfiction books and how they differ from fiction. You may display examples of nonfiction and invite children to look through them to find specific information.

Page 46: Making Groups
Learning how to complete this classification activity will help children understand the structure of analogies.

Page 47: Walk This Way
You can use the map to pose additional questions. For example: If Justina walks to and from school, how many blocks does she walk? (4) Which is farther from Justina's home, the school or the park? (park) Why do you think so? (It's one block longer.)

Page 48: A Town Map
This activity calls for students to follow directions to complete a grid. Note that there are several ways to get from Red Street and 1st Street to Green and 3rd. Encourage students to make up questions based on the grid.

Page 50: Color by Code
You may wish to review the names of the shapes on this page. Point out that some shapes appear more than once, but in different sizes.

Page 51: What Is What?
Tell students that they must observe the pictures very carefully to complete this page. Discuss their answers and encourage them to explain their thinking. You may wish to do the first problem with the class.

Page 52: Riddle Me This
Assign this page to more advanced students.

Page 53: Read First!
Take a poll on how many students followed the directions correctly. Discuss how important directions are when taking a test.

A Sorting Game

Write **P** under the plant pictures.
Write **B** under the building pictures.
Write **M** under the pictures of things that move.

1.
_____

2.
_____

3.
_____

4.
_____

5.
_____

6.
_____

7.
_____

8.
_____

9.
_____

10.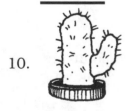
_____

11.
_____

12.
_____

Try This! **Add More** Think of one more thing for each group.

Does It Belong?

Read the word at the top of each box.
Circle the words that go with it.

1. Fruits		2. Toys	
banana	carrot	doll	yo-yo
apple	lemon	ruler	belt
bread	peach	ball	top

3. Animals		4. Tools	
lion	pear	hammer	saw
bull	stone	wrench	drill
can	monkey	leaf	book

5. Containers		6. Clothes	
box	bag	dress	sock
dog	basket	nut	hat
can	soap	skirt	robe

7. Sports		8. Meats	
movie	baseball	beef	jelly
football	tennis	pork	ham
soccer	skiing	water	hot dog

 **Try This!** **Think About It** Look at the words you didn't circle. Tell why they don't belong to that group.

Letter Code
· · · · · · · · · · · · · · · · · ·

Riddle: What is a rude carrot?

The answer is in the box, but the letters are all mixed-up!
Follow the directions below and write the new words in the blanks
to solve the riddle.

```
Q      crzph      kzgztqblz.

__   _____   _____
```

1. Change all the *z*'s to *e*'s.

2. Change all the *q*'s to *a*'s.

3. Change the *c* to *f*.

4. Change the *p* to *s*.

5. Change the *k* to *v*.

 **Try This!** **Look Again** Which letters did not change?

Which Book?

Write 1, 2, or 3 under each picture to show which book it might be in.

1.  PETS   2.  FOOD   3.  MACHINES

_____   _____   _____

_____   _____   _____

_____   _____   _____

 **Try This!**   **Add More** Think of one more thing for each group.

45

Making Groups

Read each sentence.
Find a word in the box to complete the sentence.
Write the word in the space provided.

number	hat	bed	letter
flower	bird	toy	building

1. A  is a kind of _____.

2. An  is a kind of _____.

3. A  is a kind of _____.

4. A 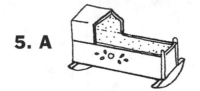 is a kind of _____.

5. A  is a kind of _____.

6. A  is a kind of _____.

7. A 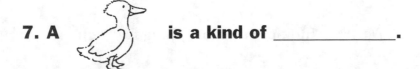 is a kind of _____.

8. A  is a kind of _____.

Try This!

Add More Think of one more thing for each group in the box.

Name _____

Walk This Way

Justina walked from her home to the library. She walked 6 blocks to get there. She rested when she was halfway there. Where do you think she rested?

How do you know?

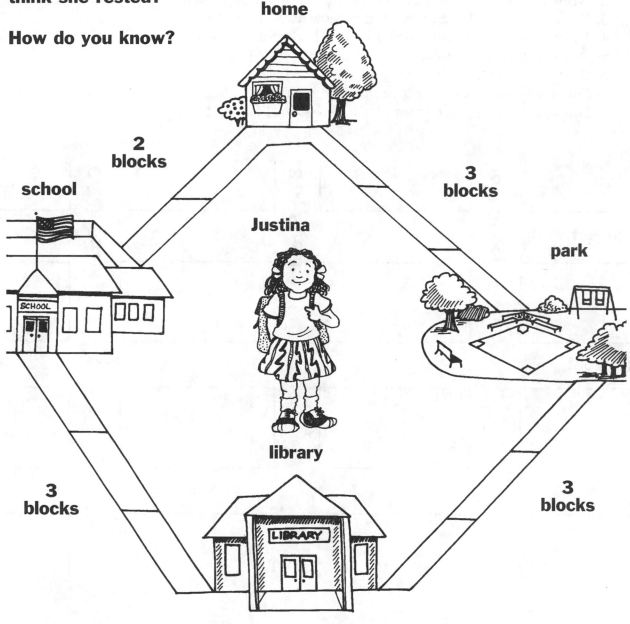

home

2 blocks

school

3 blocks

Justina

park

library

3 blocks

3 blocks

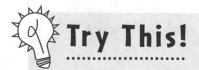 **Try This!** **Find Another Way** Trace another way that Justina can go from her home to the library.

47

A Town Map

Make a town. Follow these directions.

1. Draw a house on a corner of Red Street and 3rd Street.
2. Draw a store on a corner of Blue Street and 2nd Street.
3. Draw a tree on 1st Street, 2nd Street, and 3rd Street.
4. Draw a stop sign on a corner of Green Street and 1st Street.
5. Draw a library on a corner of 2nd Street and Red Street.
6. Draw flowers on 2nd Street.
7. Draw a firehouse on a corner of Green Street and 3rd Street.
8. Draw a school on a corner of 1st Street and Blue Street.

Red Street **Blue Street** **Green Street**

1st Street

2nd Street

3rd Street

 **Try This!** **Use the Map** Show how to get from Red Street and 1st Street to Green Street and 3rd Street.

Super Sums

· · · · · · · · · · · · · · · ·

This math-based game is a fun way for children to learn how to follow directions and categorize numbers. To play, arrange children in pairs. Each pair will need the following items:

Materials (for pair of students):

> playing cards [1 (ace) - 6 in every suit]
> paper
> pencil or pen

Directions:

1. Have each player write the numbers 1-12 on a sheet of paper.

2. Explain that the object of the game is to be the first player to cross all the numbers off the list.

3. Partners take turns picking two cards and adding up the numbers on them.

4. Partners then cross off numbers on their list. Depending on students' level, you can have them cross off the number representing the total value of the sum or two or three numbers that make the sum. For example, if a player picks a 5 and a 6, the player crosses off 11. More advanced students might also choose to cross 5 and 6, or 7 and 4, or 8 and 3, or 9 and 2, or 10 and 1, or 1, 2, and 8.

5. After each round, encourage players to share their strategies for success.

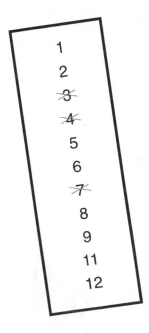

Color by Code

Read the color words.
Then color each shape.

1.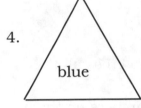

2.

3. red

4. blue

5.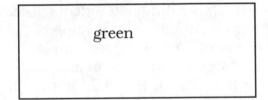
brown

6. green

Now color the picture. Use the same color for each shape as you did above.

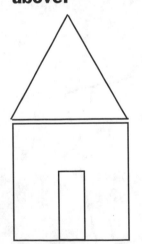
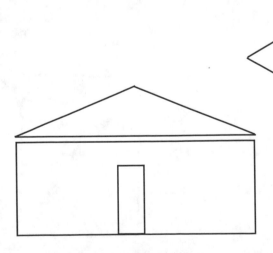
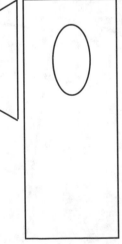

 **Try This!** **Take Another Look** Which color did you use the most? Why?

What Is What?

Read the words in each box.
Look at the pictures in each box.
Then follow the directions.

These are vehicles.

These are not vehicles.

Color the vehicles.

These are zorks.

These are not zorks.

Color the zorks.

These are tombats.

These are not tombats.

Color the tombats.

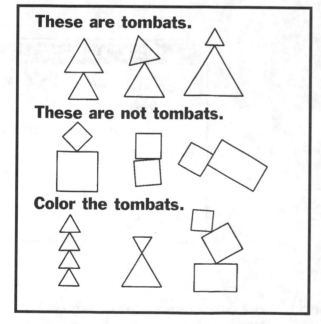

These are lorks.

These are not lorks.

Color the lorks.

 **Try This!** Explain It Tell a classmate how you decided which pictures to color.

Riddle Me This

Here's a riddle: What can you wear but never wear out?

To solve the riddle, write a word for each clue. Then read the letters in the boxes from top to bottom to form a word. Write the riddle answer on the lines above.

1.   [__] __ __
2.   __ __ [__] __
3.   __ [__] __ __
4.   __ __ [__] __
5.   __ __ __ __ [__]

C L U E S
1. not happy
2. bump
3. one more than four
4. not hot
5. rock

ANSWER: A __ __ __ __ __

Now solve this riddle: What has 40 legs, 20 eyes, and grunts?

1.   __ [__] __ __
2.   __ __ __ [__]
3.   __ __ __ [__]
4.   __ [__] __
5.   __ [__] __ __
6.   [__] __ __ __
7.   [__] __ __ __ __ __

C L U E S
1. opposite of *go*
2. color of the sky
3. home for farm animals
4. kind of monkey
5. very small
6. female child
7. opposite of *winter*

ANSWER: __ __ __ __ __ __ __

 **Try This!** **Use the Words** Write a sentence using some of the words in the puzzles.

Read First!
• • • • • • • • • • • • • • •

Read all the directions on this page before you do anything. Read all the way to the end of the paper before you do anything.

1. Write your name on the top of this paper.

2. Write your name at the top of a blank sheet of paper.

3. Say an animal's name, like cow or pig.

4. Draw a picture of the animal you named.

5. Draw the animal's home.

6. Write the animal's name.

7. Stand up, turn around three times, and clap your hands two times.

8. Sit down and touch your left ear.

9. Stand up, touch your toes without bending your knees, and sit down.

10. Write the name of a person you like.

11. Draw a picture of that person and write the person's name.

12. Read three pages in any one of your books.

13. Pat your head.

14. Draw a picture of your classroom.

15. Write the day, month, and year.

16. Write down something you want to do this weekend.

17. Stand up, reach for the sky, and sit down.

18. Stand up, hop on your left foot four times, and sit down.

19. Draw a picture of you when you are thinking.

20. Do only step 1 and step 20. Then put your head down on the desk.

 **Try This!**
• • • • • • • • • • • • • •

Explain It Tell why it was important to read the directions carefully.

Sequencing and Predicting Activities

Two important steps in the critical-thinking process are the ability to sequence details and to predict information based on prior knowledge and context clues. The activities in this section provide opportunities to help children learn and develop these skills.

Studies have shown that children who work in pairs or small groups tend to come up with more divergent responses. Therefore, you may wish to try a collaborative approach to some of these activities. The activities listed here are especially well-suited to collaborative learning:

- End the Story
- As Easy as ABC
- 1, 2, 3
- It's About Time

Use this chart to help you identify activities to use with various curriculum areas. Instructions for teacher-led activities are on the activity pages, while notes for using the student reproducibles follow the chart.

Cross-Curricular Links

Activity	Page	Content Area
Make a Puppet	56	art
End the Story	57	language arts
Dino-Mite!	58-59	mathematics
1, 2, 3	60	mathematics/language arts
Build a Castle	61	mathematics
Words in Order	62	language arts
As Easy as ABC	63	language arts
It's About Time	64	mathematics/language arts
Busy Day	65	social studies
What Will Happen?	66	science
And Then . . .	67	science/language arts
Most Likely	68	science/social studies

Teacher Notes for Student Reproducibles

Page 56: Make a Puppet
After children complete the page by putting the steps in sequence, have them check their work by actually making the puppets. You'll need to give each student a paper bag, scissors, glue, and construction paper.

Page 57: End the Story
Children will need scissors and glue to complete this page. Ask students to describe how the items in the second panel are used in the pictures in the third panel.

Pages 58-59: Dino-Mite!
Children will need crayons, scissors, and a stapler to complete this mini-book. While the title page and the last page are marked, children will have to count the dinosaurs on each page and write the number in the space provided to determine the order in which the pages should be stapled.

Page 60: 1, 2, 3
After children complete the page, reinforce sequence skills by inviting volunteers to act out each set of sentences in order.

Page 61: Build a Castle
Pose this question: If you were building the castle with real blocks, why couldn't you start from the top? Have children demonstrate with blocks.

Page 62: Words in Order
For younger children, you may wish to make a word box with the complete words that they can refer to.

Page 63: As Easy as ABC
Discuss things that are arranged in alphabetical order (books in the library, words in a dictionary, names in a telephone book).

Page 64: It's About Time
You may review the events on the time line with students before they answer the questions. Talk about the length of time covered (a week) and the order of events.

Page 65: Busy Day
Tell students that they will need to read the map carefully before they can complete the activity. Discuss why the sequence can make a difference when Mr. Harris does his errands.

Page 66: What Will Happen?
This activity gives students a chance to make predictions based on their prior knowledge. Discuss how students could check their predictions.

Page 67: And Then . . .
The items on this page call for students to use common sense and prior knowledge in making predictions.

Page 68: Most Likely
Before students begin this page, point out that sometimes when you make predictions, there are several possible outcomes, but usually one that is more likely than the others.

Name _____

Make a Puppet
· · · · · · · · · · · · · · · · · · · ·

Number the pictures in order to show how to make a puppet.

a. _____

b. _____

c. _____

d. _____

 **Try This!** · · · · · · · · · · · · · **Tell a Friend** Describe the steps for making a paper-bag puppet.

56

End the Story

Cut out the pictures on the bottom of the page. Decide which picture goes with each story. Paste the pictures on the page. Color the pictures.

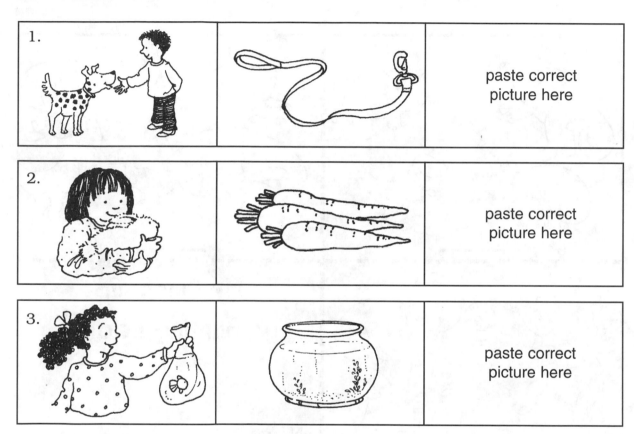

1.		paste correct picture here
2.		paste correct picture here
3.		paste correct picture here

 **Try This!** **Tell the Story** Use the pictures to tell each story.

Dino-Mite!

How many dinosaurs are on each page? Count the dinos and put the number on the line. Then cut the pages apart to make your own dino-mite counting book.

My Dinosaur
Counting Book

Name _____

The End

 **Try This!** **Color** Color the pictures in your dinosaur book.

59

1, 2, 3
. . . .

This is called sequence. Sequence is the order in which things happen.

First, you fill the tub. | Then, you put in the dog. | Finally, you wash the dog.

Read each sentence. Use the numbers 1, 2, and 3 to show the sequence.

_____ Jess went to school.

_____ Jess woke up.

_____ Jess got dressed.

_____ Kim rode down the street.

_____ Kim put on her helmet.

_____ Kim got on her bike.

_____ I get the bread.

_____ I eat lunch.

_____ I put on the jam.

 **Try This!** **Show Sequence** Draw a cartoon to show how you get ready for school.

Build a Castle

This castle needs three more rows of blocks on the bottom.
Cut out the blocks below.
Then glue as many as
you need to finish
the castle.

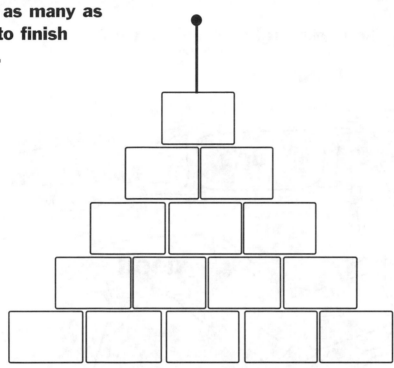

 **Try This!**

Count How many
blocks did you
add to the castle?
How many blocks
are in the castle
altogether?

Words in Order

Make an alphabet chain.
Write one letter to make a word for each link.
Begin with *a*.
Continue using the letters of the alphabet in order.

a b c d e f g h i j k l m n o p q r s t

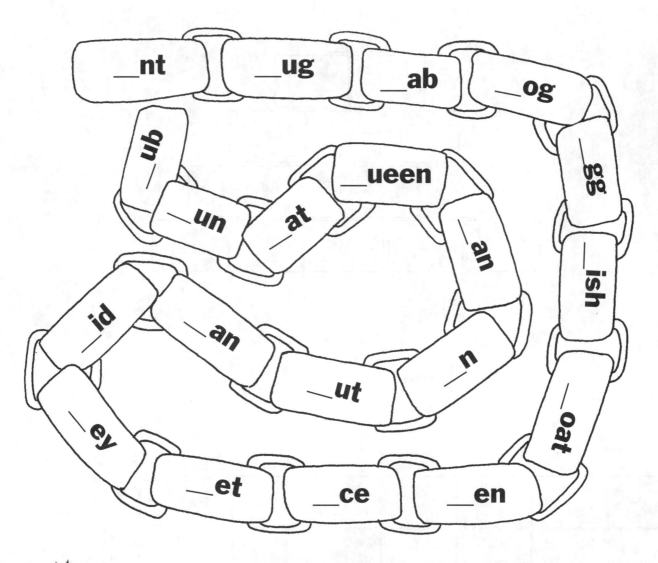

_nt   _ug   _ab   _og   _gg   _ish   _oat   _en   _ce   _et   _ey   _id   _an   _ut   _n   _an   _ueen   _at   _un   _ub

Try This! Finish the Alphabet On another sheet of paper, write a word for the letters of the alphabet that are missing here.

As Easy as ABC

Write the letters of the alphabet in order. The first and last letters are done for you.

A ____ ____ ____ ____ ____ ____ ____ ____

____ ____ ____ ____ ____ ____ ____ ____ ____

____ ____ ____ ____ ____ Z

Look at the first letter of each word. Circle the word in each pair that begins with the letter that comes first in the alphabet.

1. ape   sock   4. sun   apple
2. paper   hat   5. pen   lock
3. cow   rock   6. cat   dog

Put these words in alphabetical order.

teeth   man

dish   ape

pan   hat

lid   bird

1. _____   5. _____
2. _____   6. _____
3. _____   7. _____
4. _____   8. _____

Try This!   **More Practice** Write the letters of your name in alphabetical order.

63

It's About Time

A time line shows when things took place.
Read the time line.
Then circle the best answer.

Day 1	Day 2	Day 3	Day 4	Day 5	Day 6	Day 7
Goldie the fish is born.	Goldie learns to swim.	Goldie sees a boat.	Goldie swims into a net.	A big wave comes.	Goldie gets out!	Goldie swims away

1. When did Goldie see the boat?

    Day 1

    Day 2

    Day 3

2. When did Goldie swim into the net?

    Day 4

    Day 5

    Day 7

3. When was Goldie born?

    Day 1

    Day 4

    Day 3

4. When did Goldie get free?

    Day 2

    Day 5

    Day 6

5. How old was Goldie at the end?

    2 days old

    5 days old

    7 days old

 **Try This!** **Make a Time Line** Show five things that you did today.

Busy Day

Mr. Harris has a lot to do. Can you help him? First, read the list of things he has to do. Next, look at the map. Number the errands to show a quick order for Mr. Harris to follow. Then, draw a line on the map to show his path.

THINGS TO DO

Buy bread and eggs _____

Pick up cleaning _____

Drop off cake at school bake sale _____

Mail letters and buy stamps _____

Return Mr. Robert's wrench _____

Buy food for Sally's frog _____

Leave shoes to be fixed _____

Eat lunch at the diner _____

Try This! Look Again What other order could Mr. Harris follow?

Name _____

What Will Happen?

**What will happen to each object if you put it in water?
Draw a line to the correct words.**

fork   soap   paper

get soft

stay the same

sponge   dress

muffin   pail   noodles

**What will happen to each object if you leave it in the sun?
Draw a line to the correct words.**

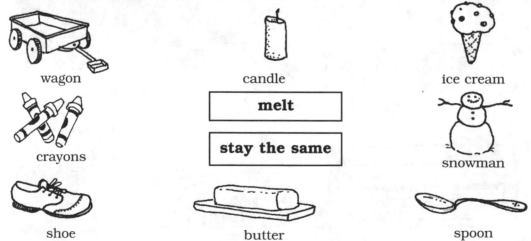

wagon   candle   ice cream

melt

stay the same

crayons   snowman

shoe   butter   spoon

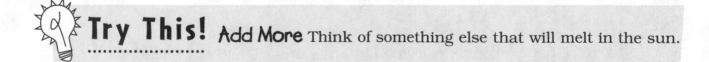

Try This! **Add More** Think of something else that will melt in the sun.

And Then . . .

Look at each picture.
Then underline the sentence that tells what will probably happen next.

a. A bear borrows the girl's suntan lotion.
b. It begins to snow.
c. The girl gets a sunburn.

a. The boy buys more food because he is still hungry.
b. The boy begins to feel sick.
c. The boy juggles the food.

a. The girl hits the ball and runs to first base.
b. The girl begins to dance.
c. The girl does a flip.

a. The boy puts the snowball in his pocket to warm it up.
b. The boy eats the snowball for lunch.
c. The boy throws the snowball to a friend.

 Try This! **Make Sense** Draw a picture of someone in the middle of an activity. Then write three sentences telling what might happen next. Two can be silly, but one must make sense. Share your work with a friend.

Most Likely

Read the beginning of each sentence.
Circle the ending you think is most likely to happen.

1. The temperature is 100. You will be

cold   warm   hot   freezing

2. Your team loses a game. You feel

disappointed   happy   silly   lucky

3. When you pack your knapsack, you will be ready for

bed   dinner   a party   school

4. When you draw a picture, you will want others to

lose it   rip it up   copy it   admire it

5. When a friend asks you to a party, you are

sad   excited   worried   sorry

6. When you practice the piano, you will

stay the same   get worse   improve   forget how to play

7. When you buy new shoes, they will be

a bigger size   an old style   the same size   a smaller size

8. When you finish dinner, you will be

hungry   ill   full   warm

 **Try This!** **Review** Look at the answers you did not circle. With your class, talk about when they might be possible.

Activities for Inferring and Drawing Conclusions

From the time they are born, children make inferences about the world around them. Through body language, sounds, and visual clues, they are able to gather information and reflect on experience. The activities in this section will help strengthen children's critical-thinking skills by developing their ability to use multisensory clues in making inferences and drawing conclusions.

You can present each activity as an independent lesson or integrate the activities into different curriculum areas as shown on the chart. You'll find the activities increase in difficulty as you work through the section. Instructions for teacher-led activities appear on the same page as the activity. Use the teacher notes that follow the chart for the student reproducibles.

Cross-Curricular Links

Activity	Page	Content Area
The Right Home	72	science
What Do I See?	73	language arts
Mystery Box	74	language arts
Magnet Studies	75	science
What Is It?	76	science/language arts
What Can You Do?	77	art
Count On	78	mathematics
Clues for Conclusions	79	language arts
Learning About the Vonce	80	science
Snap-Together Words	81	language arts
Definition Derby	82	language arts
Crack the Code	83	mathematics/language arts

Teacher Notes for Student Reproducibles

Page 72: The Right Home
Pass out crayons, scissors, and glue so children can complete the activity. Extend this activity by asking children to name or draw another possible home for each animal.

Page 75: Magnet Studies
Experimenting with magnets allows young children the freedom of trial and error and encourages them to form hypotheses. Begin by demonstrating how magnets attract certain things. Then have children complete the first column on page 75 by making predictions. Next, provide magnets and the items listed on the page and have children test their predictions and record the results. Follow up by asking children to make conclusions about what magnets attract and don't attract.

Page 76: What Is It?
This page calls for students to make inferences about the item described in each sentence. Invite children to share their own clues about classroom items for others to guess.

Page 77: What Can You Do?
Help children understand that they are tapping prior knowledge by having them tell what each item pictured is used for. After students complete the page, challenge them to use these materials to make one of the things mentioned in a sentence they underlined.

Page 79: Clues for Conclusions
Point out to students that the conclusions involve information not in the stories. For example, the first story does not say that Jack has a bike. After students have completed the page, discuss the sentences they did not circle. Why weren't these likely conclusions?

Page 80: Learning About the Vonce
You may have students work in groups to discuss their answers. Encourage them to refer to the picture and information given to defend their conclusions.

Page 81: Snap-Together Words
You may have students check their work by looking up each compound word in a dictionary.

Page 83: Crack the Code
Invite students to tell what strategies they used to crack the code.

The Right Home

Find the home for each animal.

1. Color the pictures.
2. Cut out the animals.
3. Paste each one to its home.

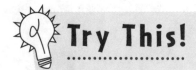 **Try This!**   **Learn More** Find out where these animals might live: beaver, horse, bee.

What Do I See?

This activity helps develop children's ability to draw inferences from verbal clues. You may wish to use it as a warm-up since it encourages children to begin reflecting on the thinking process itself.

Begin by asking students how they might describe an object—say a blimp or a dinosaur—to someone who has never seen one before. Would the name of the object alone have any meaning? Why or why not? Explore with children how they might describe the object without naming it.

Have children work with a partner. Ask one partner to make a pair of "binoculars" with his or her hands and to look through them at something they see in the classroom or outside the window. (Suggest that they choose an object that is neither too big nor too small!) Have students give their partners a series of clues that describe the object without naming it. As soon as partners have guessed the identity of the object, have students switch roles and repeat the activity.

After each round, encourage children to discuss how they figured out the mystery. Ask them to describe which clues were most effective and why. Write some of the most successful kinds of clues on the board, such as "Jonah's clue about the size of the object told me it had to be outside the window" or "Since I know the object was red, it had to be either Mark's jacket, Cindy's sweater, or the brick building across the street."

Mystery Box

This activity encourages students to examine and interpret information and then apply their knowledge to new situations.

Before class begins, make a collection of familiar objects, such as buttons, coins, and crayons. Select one object and place it in a covered shoe box. To begin the activity, tell students you have placed an object in the box. Explain that you are going to write the names of five objects on the board, and that one of the objects will be the one in the box. For beginning students, you may wish to list objects that are very different; for more advanced students, you may want to list objects that are similar.

Then invite students to guess what is in the box by asking you *yes* and *no* questions. For example, they might ask, "Is the item metal?" "Do you cut with it?" "Can I buy things with it?" Encourage students to base each successive question on the information they have gleaned from the previous question and to use the information to eliminate possibilities. Repeat the activity several times, using a different object each time. With each round, challenge students to guess the object using fewer and fewer questions.

As children become more familiar with the activity, you may wish to have them do it in small groups, with one person in each group serving as the leader. The first student to guess the object in the box becomes the group's next leader.

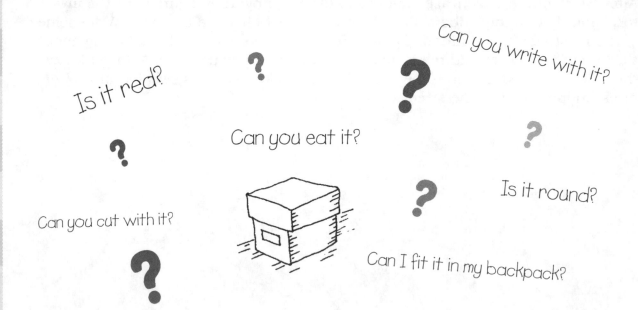

Is it red?

?

?

Can you write with it?

?

Can you eat it?

?

?

Is it round?

Can you cut with it?

?

Can I fit it in my backpack?

Magnet Studies

Look at each thing on the list. Will a magnet pick it up? Put a check under *yes* or *no* to tell your prediction. Then, use a magnet to check your prediction, and put a check under *yes* or *no* in the results column.

	Prediction		Results	
	Yes	No	Yes	No
1. Pencil				
2. Plastic ruler				
3. Piece of wood				
4. Crayon				
5. Pipe cleaner				
6. Pin				
7. Nickel				
8. Nail				
9. Rubber band				
10. Your hand				

Try This! THINK ABOUT IT How are the things that magnets will pick up alike?

75

Name _____

What Is It?

Read the sentences.
Look at the pictures.
Write the number of the sentence under the picture it tells about.

1. It purrs but is not a good pet.
2. It is yellow and likes the sun.
3. It barks but is not a dog.
4. It changes its shape during the month.
5. It is a good home for birds.
6. It stings, but don't take it personally.
7. It runs fast and loves nuts.
8. It looks fluffy but is wet inside.

_____ _____ _____ _____

_____ _____ _____ _____

 **Try This!** Play a Game Choose something in the room. Give your classmates a sentence clue. Can they guess what it is?

What Can You Do?

**Look at the things that Kia has.
Then read the sentences.
If Kia can use all three things
to do a job, underline the sentence.**

1. She could make her bed.

2. She could make a banner.

3. She could design a card.

4. She could clean her glasses.

5. She could make a drawing.

6. She could make a mini-book.

7. She could decorate a box.

8. She could set the table.

 **Try This!** **Look Again** Look at the sentences you didn't under-
line. Tell what you would need to do these jobs.

Count On

Counting money is a challenging skill because it involves drawing conclusions based on counting by ones, fives, and tens. This usually does not come easily to children until about the third grade. This activity will help children in grades 1–3 learn critical-thinking strategies to draw conclusions about numbers.

Materials for each team:

- a number cube
- 10 pennies, 10 nickels

Note: You can use play money or real coins for this activity.

Directions:

1. Arrange children in teams and explain that the object of the game is to be the first player to earn 20 cents. To earn the money, players have to match the value of the coin to the amount on the number cube.

2. The first player rolls the number cube and takes the number of pennies it shows.

3. The second player rolls the number cube and takes the number of pennies shown. Players continue by alternating turns.

4. As each player accumulates 5 pennies or more, the player trades 5 pennies for a nickel.

5. The first player to accumulate 20 cents wins.

6. You can vary the amount players have to accumulate and add other coins, such as dimes and quarters.

Clues for Conclusions

When you read, you sometimes draw conclusions. You put together clues from the story and things you already know. The result is your conclusion. In a way, it's like adding 1 + 1 = 2.

story clues + what you know = conclusions

Read the stories. Circle the best conclusions.

1. Jack put on his helmet. He put up the kickstand. He looked both ways down the street. He backed out of the driveway.

    Conclusion: It was night.
    It was raining.
    Jack was on his bike.
    Jack was in bed.

2. Lisa helped Kim spell the word *green*. They left their desks and got in line. Lisa and Kim went to the playground. They played ball.

    Conclusion: Lisa and Kim are at home.
    Lisa and Kim are in school.
    Lisa is not a good speller.
    Lisa and Kim are on a plane.

3. Sam took out the bread. Then he got the jam, a plate, and a knife. Sam washed his hands.

    Conclusion: Sam is going fishing.
    Sam is cleaning up.
    Sam is alone in the house.
    Sam is making a sandwich.

 **Try This!** **Check Your Conclusions** Reread each story. Underline the clues that helped you draw a conclusion.

Learning About the Vonce

Here's a Vonce. It is a make-believe animal. The Vonce has two short front legs. Its front feet have sharp claws. Its back feet are webbed. Its tail is short and furry. Its body has thick fur. The fur is brown in the summer and white in the winter. The Vonce has big, round ears. It has a long nose. Its eyes are very small. Its teeth are very sharp.

What can you tell about the Vonce by the way it looks?

1. Do you think it is cold where the Vonce lives? _____

   Explain your answer. _____

2. Do you think the Vonce can swim? _____

   Explain your answer. _____

3. Do you think the Vonce can climb trees? _____

   Explain your answer. _____

4. Do you think the Vonce can hear well? _____

   Explain your answer. _____

5. Do you think the Vonce can run fast? _____

   Explain your answer. _____

Try This!

Write Write a story about the Vonce. Use the information on this page and your answers to help you.

Snap-Together Words

**Sometimes you can figure out a new word by looking at its parts.
Follow these steps with the word sunshine:**

1. See if the word has two or more parts.   sun   shine

2. Say each part.   sun   shine

3. Think what each part means.   sun = light
shine = bright

4. Put the parts together again.   sunshine

Figure out what each of these words means.

1. backyard   _____

2. teacup   _____

3. billfold   _____

4. barnyard   _____

5. airline   _____

6. tiptoe   _____

7. raindrop   _____

8. sunrise   _____

9. campground   _____

10. masterpiece   _____

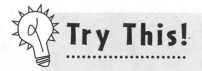 **Try This!** **Use What You Learn** On another sheet of paper, write a sentence using each word.

Definition Derby

In this activity, children infer a word's meaning through the use of context clues. Read the following sentences to the class and ask students to define the underlined word. (You may wish to reproduce the sentences so that more assured readers can follow along as you read.) As each word is defined, have children explain how they inferred its meaning. Which clues in each sentence proved to be most helpful?

1. The ancient building was built a long, long time ago.
2. Have they captured the tiger that escaped from the zoo?
3. How did Marc reply to the question?
4. You can cut your lip on a broken cup rim.
5. The clown made Maria feel more cheerful.
6. It was damp outside after the rain.
7. The light was so faint I could hardly see.
8. Luke could not drink the milk because it was spoiled.
9. Chris seized the toy from his sister.
10. They chatted so much that their teacher had to tell them to keep quiet.
11. Henry tried to conceal his braces by closing his mouth.
12. The room was vacant after all the children left.
13. Mrs. Smith tried to coax her daughter into drinking her milk.
14. The teacher asked Charles to fetch the books from the cupboard.
15. The kids loathe liver and spinach.
16. The agile tumbler could touch her nose to her knees.
17. D.J. wanted to assemble the kit on his own.
18. Because they were not in a hurry, the girls ambled home slowly after school.
19. The sponge was so moist that it was dripping.
20. The space between the earth and the sun is very vast.
21. The wrecking crane was set to demolish the office.
22. My mother's fingers are so nimble that she can untie any knot.
23. Put a sweater on because it is chilly tonight.
24. The flexible tube bent easily.
25. The child's hands were grimy after he played in the dirt.

Crack the Code

Find the secret word! Each letter stands for a number. Write the number for each letter.

Like this:

___	___	___	___
0	1	2	3

$A + A = R$ **Did you find the code?**
$R + P = R$ $0 = P$ $1 = A$ $2 = R$ $3 = K$
$A + R = K$ The word is PARK.

Crack this code.

1.
___	___	___	___
0	1	2	3

$B + E = E$
$A + E = R$
$R - A = E$

2.
___	___	___	___
0	1	2	3

$D - B = D$
$R + I = D$
$I + I = R$

3.
___	___	___	___
0	1	2	3

$I + I = M$
$M + I = E$
$E - D = E$

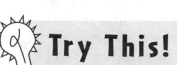 **Try This!** **Do the Math** Write each code clue as an addition or subtraction sentence with numbers.

Evaluating Activities

Before children begin the activities in this section, explain that *evaluating* means "making a judgment about something." Point out that people often make evaluations in their everyday life—judgments about other people, events, and things they see; foods they eat; and books they read. Invite volunteers to share an evaluation they made today.

The activities in this section will guide children through the process of evaluating. You can use each activity as a complete lesson or weave the activities into other curriculum studies. Within this section, the activities are arranged from easiest to most difficult. Instructions for teacher-led activities appear on the same page as the activity. Teacher notes for the student reproducibles follow the chart.

Cross-Curricular Links

Activity	Page	Content Area
The Sky Is Falling!	86	language arts
Be an Editor	87	language arts
Class Flag	88	social studies/art
Pet Shopping	89	science
The Perfect Day	90	language arts/mathematics
Will It Fit?	91	mathematics
Food Ratings	92	health/science
Favorite Things	93	mathematics
Pick a Winner	94	language arts
Think About It	95	social studies/language arts
Thumbs Up, Thumbs Down	96	language arts
Pitch In!	97	science

Teacher Notes for Student Reproducibles

Page 87: Be an Editor
This activity not only provides an opportunity to exercise judgment, but helps students focus on the concept of a main idea in a paragraph. Learning how to delete unrelated or redundant sentences is important to the revision process in writing as well. Have students explain their reasoning for each sentence they drew a line through.

Page 89: Pet Shopping
Invite students to share their pet evaluations, stressing that these may differ because not everyone makes the same judgments.

Page 90: The Perfect Day
Use the data from students' pages to make a class graph showing favorite and least favorite activities.

Page 91: Will It Fit?
In this activity students make judgments about size. You can extend this activity by displaying other containers and asking children to judge whether or not certain objects will fit in them. Discuss how children can check to see if their judgments are correct.

Page 92: Food Ratings
Use the data on students' pages to compile a list of the three favorite class foods. You might also use this opportunity to discuss the importance of healthful foods.

Page 93: Favorite Things
Ask students what conclusions they can draw from the results on their pages. For example, can they conclude that one sport is less popular in your class than others?

Page 94: Pick a Winner
Have children work with a partner to complete this page. Then bring the class together to find out which was the most common answer for each question.

Page 96: Thumbs Up, Thumbs Down
Compile students' pages into a class resource folder. List the names of the books covered on the outside of the folder. Encourage students to check the folder when they are choosing a book to read.

The Sky Is Falling!

A good way to develop children's ability to evaluate is through a literature-based approach. Obtain a version of "Chicken Little" or "The Three Sillies." Both of these stories are about characters who draw absurd conclusions from scant evidence. Read one or both of the stories to the class. Then lead a class discussion focusing on the following questions:

• What did the characters believe would happen?
• What evidence did they have?
• Was it enough evidence?
• How else might they have interpreted the situation?
• What else might they have done? What would you have done?
• Do you think the way they acted was silly? Why or why not?
• What did the characters' behavior tell you about them?

Then challenge students to come up with their own tales based on characters who jump to conclusions without carefully evaluating the evidence. Have children work in small groups to brainstorm their ideas. You might also have students perform their stories as skits.

Be an Editor

Read each paragraph.
Find a sentence that you would take out.
Draw a line through that sentence.

1. Mr. Mendez has a blue tie. It is made of silk. His belt is brown. He wears this tie on special days.

2. My brother and I have bunk beds. We have bunk beds. He sleeps on the top. I have the bottom.

3. Aunt Vicky loves her garden. She plants bulbs in the fall. In the spring she does a lot of weeding. Her cookies are great.

4. This is a beaver dam. The beavers made it. It is made of logs and mud. The beavers cut down the logs with their teeth.

 **Try This!** **Write a Paragraph** Write a paragraph about the room where you sleep. Reread it to make sure that all the sentences fit.

Class Flag

Brainstorm a list of important items in the classroom with your class. Then have children suggest ideas or concepts that are important in the classroom. Write students' suggestions on the board.

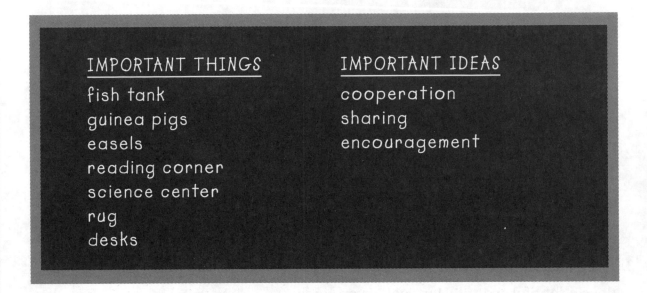

IMPORTANT THINGS
fish tank
guinea pigs
easels
reading corner
science center
rug
desks

IMPORTANT IDEAS
cooperation
sharing
encouragement

Explain to students that they are going to make a class flag. Point out that the colors and designs on a flag usually tell something about the nation or organization it represents. Ask students if they know what the stars and stripes and the red, white, and blue colors on the American flag mean. Invite students to mention other flags they may be familiar with and ask volunteers to talk about the flags they may have made in organizations such as the 4-H or the Scouts.

Suggest to students that their class flag tell something about what their class is like and what makes it special. Divide the class into small groups. Ask children to look at the items on the board—adding any additional ones they want—and then to create a design for a flag. Encourage children to work cooperatively to design and color their flag.

When everyone is finished, have each group display its flag and explain what each of the items represents. Children may also wish to write brief descriptions of their flags. Display the flags in a prominent place so everyone can enjoy them.

Pet Shopping

What kind of pet would you like to have?
List some things that make each animal a good pet.
Then list some reasons that the animal might not be a good pet.

	Good Pet	Not a Good Pet
Cat		
Ant		
Parrot		
Elephant		
Snake		

Try This! **Keep Thinking** Think of another animal that you believe would be a good pet. Write two sentences explaining why.

89

Name _____

The Perfect Day

The pictures show some things you can do in a day.
Think of three more things. Write them on the lines.
Next, circle five things you did this week.
List these things in order on the chart—from your most favorite to
your least favorite.

_____   _____   _____

Most Favorite   Least Favorite

 Try This! **Choose Your Favorite** What is the thing you like to
do the most? Write a sentence to tell why.

90

Will It Fit?

Circle the items on the right that will fit in the container to the left.

1.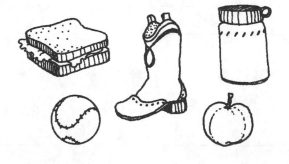

2.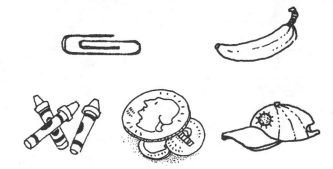

3.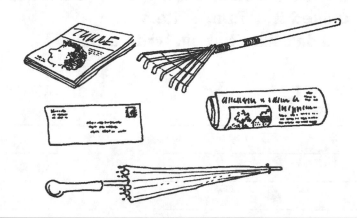

 Try This! Draw and Think On another sheet of paper, draw a picture of a container that is diffrent from the ones above. List 5 things that could fit in it.

Food Ratings

List all of the foods you ate yesterday.
If you liked the food a lot, write a **1** next to it.
If you liked it a little, write a **2**.
If you didn't like it at all, write a **3**.

BREAKFAST

_____

_____

_____

_____

_____

_____

LUNCH

_____

_____

_____

_____

_____

_____

DINNER

_____

_____

_____

_____

_____

SNACKS

_____

_____

_____

_____

_____

My favorite food of all was _____.

 **Try This!** **Eat a New Food** Think of a food you've never had.
Try it and then rate it 1, 2, or 3.

Name _____

Favorite Things

Do your friends all like the same things?
Take a poll using the lists below.
Ask 4 friends which things they like best. Write their names on the lines provided and circle their answers.

NAME	COLOR	FOOD	SPORT
1. _____	red	fruit	soccer
	blue	vegetables	baseball
	green	pasta	swimming
	yellow	bread	skating
2. _____	red	fruit	soccer
	blue	vegetables	baseball
	green	pasta	swimming
	yellow	bread	skating
3. _____	red	fruit	soccer
	blue	vegetables	baseball
	green	pasta	swimming
	yellow	bread	skating
4. _____	red	fruit	soccer
	blue	vegetables	baseball
	green	pasta	swimming
	yellow	bread	skating

Look at the answers.
Write the most popular choice for each group.

Color_____   Food_____   Sport_____

 **Try This!** Take Another Poll Ask 4 more friends what color, food, and sport they like best. Compare the results from both polls. Do the favorites change?

Pick a Winner

Read each sentence.
Circle the word you think best answers the question.

1. Which is the best pet?   tiger   bear   bird   moth

2. What keeps you warm?   milk   pen   coat   tree

3. Which is fastest?   fish   turtle   car   plane

4. Which is coldest?   ice   carrots   dog's nose   pea

5. Which is slowest?   bird   worm   jet   train

6. Which is nearest?   star   ground   clouds   sun

7. Which is deepest?   pond   puddle   ocean   tub

8. Which is brightest?   lamp   sun   penny   moon

9. Which is biggest?   banana   ear   dime   toe

10. Which is the softest?   hill   pillow   ice   rock

Sit with a friend. Talk about your answers. Explain why you chose them.

 **Try This!** **Discuss** Why are some questions easier to agree on than others? Talk over your ideas with a classmate.

Think About It

This activity calls for students to think carefully about generalizations. Write an example such as the following on the chalkboard:

All people who go to a pool know how to swim.

Read the statement with students and ask them if it is true.
Ask: Is it always true? Encourage students to give an example of when it might not be true. For instance:

A baby doesn't know how to swim.

Then ask students to reword the sentence so it is true. For example:

Most people who go to a pool know how to swim.

Give the following statements one by one. Challenge students to first think of a sentence to prove that the statement is not always true. Then have them think of a way to reword the orignal sentence. Discuss their responses. Point out that often statements of this kind include words such as *all, always,* and *everyone,* whereas statements using words such as *most* or *some* allow for other possibilties.

1. All teachers are women.

2. Everyone who works takes a train.

3. All doctors wear white coats.

4. Students are always hungry after school.

5. All bus drivers are men.

6. Tests are always on Friday.

Name _____

Thumbs Up, Thumbs Down

Pick a book you read a short time ago. Tell what you think about it by answering these questions by circling either a thumbs up, or a thumbs down.

Thumbs up = yes   Thumbs down = no

1. What is the title?

_____

2. Who is the author?

3. Did you like the way the book started?
   Write a sentence to explain your answer.

4. Did you like the characters?
   Write a sentence to explain your answer.

5. Did you like the illustrations?
   Write a sentence to explain your answer.

6. Did you like the story ending?
   Write a sentence to explain your answer.

7. Would you tell a friend to read this book?
   Write a sentence to explain your answer.

Try This! **Review a Book** On another sheet of paper, write a review of your book. Use the answers on this page to help you.

Pitch In!

This activity helps children focus on how to best use their time and resources to protect the environment. After they have completed their evaluation, children might create and implement a plan suited to their abilities and goals.

Begin by exploring some of the different things children can do—both as individuals or as a class—to help the environment. Some class possibilities might include picking up litter on the playground, recycling paper in the classroom, recycling plastic and glass in the cafeteria, feeding wild birds in the winter, making posters to remind others to help out.

Write each idea on the chalkboard. Ask children to list pros and cons for carrying it out.

Next, divide the class into small groups. Have each group evaluate the possible ideas as a class project. Or you may wish to assign one project to each group to evaluate. Ask the groups to make a recommendation to the class telling whether or not the project would work. Then, have the class vote on all the ideas that were well recommended. Finally, have students draw up a plan for the project they have chosen.

As students work, they may want to contact the following agencies for suggestions and resources:

Center for Environmental Information, Inc.
99 Court Street,
Rochester, NY 14604   (716) 546-3796

CEI is a nonprofit organization that provides materials concerning environmental and conservation issues. Information is free.

Children of the Green Earth
307 N. 48th Street,
Seattle, WA 98103   (206) 781-0852

CGE, a nonprofit organization, encourages students to "regreen" the earth by planting trees and caring for forests.

The Cousteau Society
930 W 21st Street,
Norfolk, VA 23517   (804) 627-1144

The Cousteau Society runs a number of programs and disseminates information on environmental issues. Dolphin Log is a bimonthly magazine with stories, games, facts, and experiments for children ages seven and up.

Earth Island Institute
300 Broadway, Suite 28,
San Francisco, CA 94133   (415) 788-3666

This nonprofit organization develops and supports innovative activities to restore and preserve the environment.

Kids Against Pollution
PO Box 775,
Closter, NJ 07624   (201) 784-0668

Created by a group of elementary school children from New Jersey, KAP is an excellent source of information on what children can do in their schools, homes, and communities to help the environment. Yearly membership is $6.00.

National Recycling Coalition, Inc.
1101 30th Street, NW, Suite 305,
Washington, DC 20007   (202) 625-6406

NRC, a nonprofit organization, runs a number of programs, including Peer Match, which provides assistance to communities wishing to implement recycling programs.

Analyzing Activities

Ask children if they have ever been faced with a very tricky problem—something they couldn't solve easily. It might have been a problem in math, difficulty finding a lost item, or a problem deciding how to make the best use of their time.

Point out that no matter what the problem, a good way to solve it is to analyze it. Explain that analyzing a problem means breaking it down into smaller parts or "steps" and then thinking about each one. Tell children that when they analyze a problem this way, they are better able to predict possible outcomes and propose solutions that make sense.

After you have discussed this process, you may wish to model it by working through some of the activities in this section. Consider using these activities:
• Guess the Rule (p. 102)
• Apart and Together (p. 103)
• Some Solutions (p. 104)
• Does It Rhyme? (p. 108).
After you have finished modeling the activity, ask children to comment on the way you arrived at your solution.

The chart shows related curriculum areas for each activity. Use the teacher notes that follow to introduce the student reproducibles.

Cross-Curricular Links

Activity	Page	Content Area
Finish the Picture	100	mathematics/art
What Is Missing?	101	mathematics
Guess the Rule	102	language arts
Apart and Together	103	language arts
Some Solutions	104	social studies/science
Mystery Word	105	language arts
Real or Make-Believe?	106	language arts
Alike and Different	107	science/mathematics
Does It Rhyme?	108	language arts
If I Were a...	109	language arts
Double Fun	110	language arts
What's the Meaning?	111	language arts
Ha! Ha!	112	language arts
Solve It	113	science

Teacher Notes for Student Reproducibles

Page 100: Finish the Picture
Children must determine what is missing in each picture before they can finish it. Discuss the concept of parts of a whole.

Page 101: What Is Missing?
In this activity, which builds on page 100, students complete a sentence to describe what is missing from each picture.

Page 103: Apart and Together
You may wish to brainstorm reasons for friends beforehand. Write students' ideas on the chalkboard so they can refer to them as they complete the page.

Page 106: Real or Make-Believe?
Many children have difficulty differentiating real events from imagined ones. Before passing out this page, you might discuss examples of familiar make-believe storybook and cartoon characters.

Page 107: Alike and Different
Extend the activity by having children compare things that have more similarities than a shark and a cat. For example, you may compare two kinds of cats—a tiger and a lion.

Page 108: Does It Rhyme?
You may wish to review short and long vowel sounds before introducing this activity.

Page 109: If I Were a . . .
Extend the activity by asking children to write a story about their life as one of the items on the page.

Page 110: Double Fun
Encourage students to explain how they know what meaning is being used in each sentence.

Page 111: What's the Meaning?
This page focuses on common idioms in the English language. Since these are difficult for many children, and particularly so for students whose first language is not English, you may wish to compile a longer list for class study.

Page 112: Ha! Ha!
Point out that jokes and riddles are based on multiple word meanings. Invite students to share the riddles they make up.

Page 113: Solve It
Encourage children to be creative in their solutions. For example, if someone says that you could tap something off a high shelf with a broom, accept that as a possible answer.

Name _____

Finish the Picture
....

What is each picture missing?
Draw the missing part on each picture.

1.

2.

3.

4.

5.

6.

7.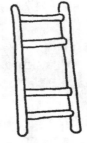

8.

 Try This! Color Color your finished pictures.

What Is Missing?

Read each sentence.
Study the picture.
Complete the sentence to tell what is missing.

1.    The clock is missing a _____.

2.    The rabbit is missing an _____.

3.    The duck is missing a _____.

4.    The wagon is missing a _____.

5. 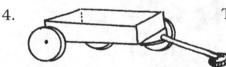   The pitcher is missing a _____.

6.    The shoe is missing a _____.

 Try This! Finish the Pictures Draw the missing part on each picture.

Guess the Rule

In this game children use analysis to figure out a rule. Explain that you are going to think of a rule and they have to guess what it is.

Seat children in a circle. Think of a simple rule such as "you must wear the color red," or "You must wear a T-shirt with writing on it." Without telling the class what the rule is, point to the children who fit the rule and have them take a place in the center of the circle. Instruct the rest of the class to analyze those in the circle to see what they might have in common. Invite children to guess your rule.

The child who guesses the rule correctly can think of a new rule for the next round. You may suggest that children confine their rules to items of clothing or other belongings.

What do these children have in common?

(They are all wearing high-top sneakers.)

Name _____

Apart and Together

Friends mean a lot. On each piece of the puzzle, write one reason why you think friends are important. One is done for you.

Friends help each other.

Now cut your puzzle apart. Work with a friend to put it back together.

Try This! **Share Your Ideas** Tell the rest of the class why you think friends are important.

Some Solutions

Present each of the following situations to the entire class, or have students work in small groups. Ask students to analyze each situation and then to suggest their solutions. Discuss students' proposals.

1. Two friends want to play with the same toy. How can they solve their problems without fighting?

2. If you lost your mittens, how could you keep your hands warm?

3. You're on a day-long hike, and you get an idea for a story you have to write for school. You don't have a pencil or paper with you to take notes. What could you do to remember your idea until you get home?

4. You've just moved to a new town, and it's your birthday. How should you celebrate?

5. If you were outside and it began to rain, what would you do to keep dry?

6. It's time to go to sleep, but your bed disappeared. What will you do?

7. List things you could do if you were invisible that you can't do now.

8. How could you keep a snowman from melting?

9. If your ball got stuck on the school roof, how would you get it down?

10. How could you wash the outside of these windows from the inside?

Mystery Word

Listening for specific sounds in words helps children develop both analyzing and decoding skills. Begin this activity by telling children that you are going to name a group of things and read some words that belong to that group. Explain that students are to listen carefully to identify the mystery word in each group. The clue to the mystery word will be a vowel sound.

Slowly read aloud these categories and the words that follow them. Direct children to listen well and write the word in each group that has the long *e* sound as in *bee* and *seat* .

People: you, us, we, them (*we*)
Vegetables: lettuce, beans, carrots, corn (*beans*)
Body Parts: hands, toes, nose, feet (*feet*)
Colors: red, blue, yellow, green (*green*)
Insects: fly, wasp, ant, bee (*bee*)

Continue the same activity with the short *a* sound as in *nap.*

People: girl, Bill, man, they (*man*)
Vegetables: peas, potatoes, carrots, tomatoes (*carrots*)
Body Parts: hand, brain, knee, neck (*hand*)
Colors: pink, blue, black, white (*black*)
Clothing: coat, mittens, hat, sweater (*hat*)

You can use this activity to help children analyze any sound you are reviewing or introducing.

Name _____

Real or Make-Believe?

Some things are real, and others are make-believe.

Real  **Make-Believe**

Read each sentence. Write *yes* if it is real. Write *no* if it is make-believe.

_____ 1. The [fish] drank a [glass] of milk.

_____ 2. The [bee] flew around the [flowers].

_____ 3. The [cow] jumped over the [moon].

_____ 4. The [boy] walked to [school].

_____ 5. The [mouse] ate some [cheese].

_____ 6. The [tree] talked to the [banana].

_____ 7. The [cat] barked.

_____ 8. The [dog] went swimming.

_____ 9. The [plate] ran away with the [sandwich].

_____ 10. The [girl] set the [table].

Try This! Explain Tell the class your reason for each sentence that you wrote *No*.

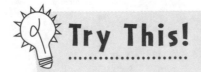

106

Name _____

Alike and Different
· ·

How are things the same? How are they different? You can show this with a chart:

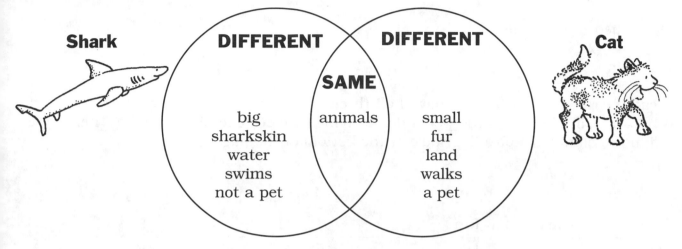

Shark

DIFFERENT   DIFFERENT

SAME

big	animals	small
sharkskin		fur
water		land
swims		walks
not a pet		a pet

Cat

Fill in this chart to show how a bicycle and a rocket are alike and different.

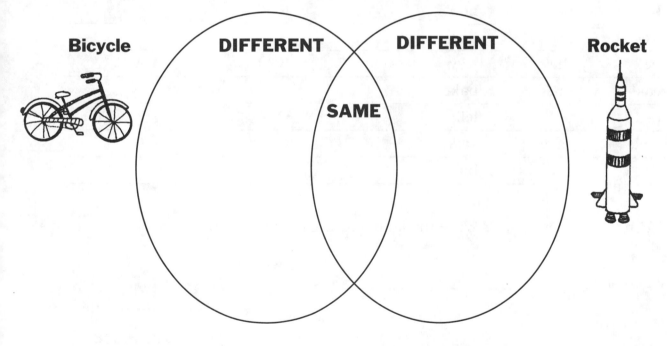

Bicycle

DIFFERENT   DIFFERENT

SAME

Rocket

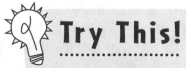

Try This! · · · · · · · · · · · ·

Read Find a book about sharks and one about cats. Read to learn more about how these animals are alike and different.

Does It Rhyme?

Words rhyme when they have the same sound. Here are words that rhyme:

hen	men	pen	ten	den
in	bin	win	pin	shin

Read the three words in each row. If **all** three words rhyme, circle the letter under *Yes*. If **all** three of the words don't rhyme, circle the letter under *No*. Then fill in the blanks to solve the riddle at the bottom of the page.

			Yes	No
sun	run	fun	H	P
big	me	lake	L	E
fig	see	we	Q	A
top	pop	hop	R	M
frog	log	hog	S	S
he	they	saw	K	A
cake	make	bake	Y	N
bell	tell	fell	O	E
took	gave	save	C	L
dog	cat	bird	V	K

When does a hen laugh? Write the letters in the order that they appear above to solve the riddle.

When she ___ ___ ___ ___ ___

___

___ ___ ___ ___

Try This!

Rhyme Some More
Think of another word to add to each group of rhyming words.

If I Were a . . . .

Sometimes it's fun to pretend. When you pretend, you use your imagination. Use your imagination to answer these questions.

1. If I were an animal, I would be a _____

because_____.

2. If I were a color, I would be the color _____

because_____.

3. If I were a place, I would be _____

because_____.

4. If I were a tree I would be a _____

because_____.

5. If I were a toy I would be a _____

because_____.

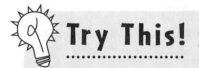 **Try This!** Draw a Picture Choose one of the things you pretended to be. Draw a picture to show how you would look!

Double Fun

What's a hat? You know! It's something you wear on your head! A hat is a hat.

But some words have more than one meaning. The word *park,* for example, has two meanings.

park – a place with trees   park – to pull over

Write the meaning for each underlined word.

1. I look at my <u>watch</u> to see the time. _____

2. I like to <u>watch</u> baseball. _____

3. You need a <u>bat</u> to play baseball. _____

4. The <u>bat</u> flew in the barn window. _____

5. He <u>leaves</u> the house late. _____

6. The <u>leaves</u> fall off the tree. _____

7. I <u>point</u> to the bird. _____

8. We scored a <u>point</u>! _____

 **Try This!** **More Double Fun** On another sheet of paper, draw two pictures to show two different meanings for the word *fly.*

What's the Meaning?

People often use sayings when they speak. Sometimes the meaning of a word changes in a saying.

Color the picture that shows what each saying means.

1. Rosa cracked up.

2. He worked around the clock.

Now draw a picture to show what these sayings mean.

3. Sid ran into a friend.

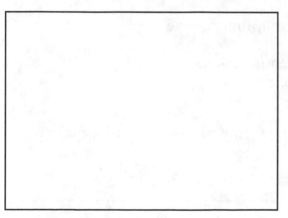

4. Jill is down in the dumps.

 **Try This!** **Find More** Make a list of other sayings that you know. Write what each one means.

Ha! Ha!
• • • • • • • • • • •

Do you like riddles? A riddle is a question with a funny answer. Here are some riddles:

Why did the man throw the clock out the window?

He wanted to see time fly!

Where do you find the world's biggest spider?

In the World Wide Web.

Draw a line from each riddle to its answer.

Question

1. What do sea monsters eat for lunch?

2. Why don't fish go near computers?

3. Why do ducks fly south?

4. What mouse won't eat cheese?

Answer

a. They're afraid of getting caught in the Internet.

b. Fish and ships

c. A computer mouse

d. Because it's too far to walk

 **Try This!** **Write a Riddle** Write a funny answer of your own to these questions.

1. Why do bees hum? _____

_____

2. What's more amazing than a talking dog? _____

_____

Solve It

· · · · · · · · · · ·

Some problems have only one answer. Some problems have many answers.

Each sentence tells about a problem.
The picture shows one way to solve it.
Think of your own solution and draw a picture to show what it is.

1. Jed spilled his milk.

2. Penny lost her umbrella.

3. Wendy can't reach her game.

4. The lightbulb in Paco's lamp burned out.

 **Try This!**
· · · · · · · · · · · · · · · ·

Share Show your picture solutions to a friend.
How would your friend solve the same problem?

Synthesizing Activities

Explain that *synthesizing* means "putting it all together." Tell children that in these activities they will get a chance to use what they know to figure out new things. Encourage children to take their time and think carefully as they work.

Many of these activities are ideally suited to cooperative groups. If you decide to group children, make sure that everyone has a specific task to perform—one that is suited to the child's skills, strengths, and interests. Pages that lend themselves to this approach are:

- The Play's the Thing (p. 117)
- Games Galore (p. 119)
- Use It Well (p. 120)

Use the chart to help you identify activities that tie in with other content areas. Use the teacher notes that follow to introduce the student reproducibles.

Cross-Curricular Links

Activity	Page	Content Area
It's Show Time!	116	language arts
The Play's the Thing	117	language arts
Build a Tale	118	language arts
Games Galore	119	social studies
Use It Well	120	art/science
Paint a Rainbow	121	art/science
Shape Pictures	122	mathematics
Fishy Stuff	123	science
Story Time	124	language arts

Teacher Notes for Student Reproducibles

Page 120: Use It Well
This page, which calls for students to propose alternative uses for common materials, builds on the activity on page 119. Have children work in groups to brainstorm ideas for each item. Then bring the groups together to present their proposals.

Page 121: Paint a Rainbow

Students will need brushes and paint to complete this page. You might want to spread old newspapers on desks or tabletops before students begin experimenting.

Page 122: Shape Pictures

Students may use the shapes on this page as patterns and cut them out from colored paper. Or consider mounting children's shape pictures on colored paper. Be sure to display the finished pictures in the classroom.

Page 124: Story Time

You may have students work with a peer partner to discuss their ideas for story problems and endings. Encourage students to write out their complete stories on separate sheets of paper. Younger students may dictate their stories. If you have a computer in the room, students can type their stories on it and print out copies.

It's Show Time!

One of the most effective ways to teach students the critical-thinking skill of synthesizing is through dramatics. Drama also encourages students to express themselves creatively and to work cooperatively in a group.

Pantomime involves actions without words. This form of creative dramatics challenges children to convey ideas in an unaccustomed form of communication.

Here are ten pantomimes you can give children. Write the scenarios on slips of paper and have volunteers choose one to act out. Invite the rest of the class to guess the action.

1. You are a detective trying to solve a crime.

2. You are a baby bird that has just hatched.

3. You are a giant looking down on people.

4. You are a doll that comes alive.

5. You are a robot that walks and talks.

6. You are a tightrope walker in a circus.

7. You are a puppet on a string.

8. You are an explorer in a strange new country.

9. You are a scary dinosaur.

10. You are a flower that is ready to bloom.

The Play's the Thing

Here are some creative dramatics you can use to help children develop their synthesizing skills. Students can work on the following activities in pairs, small groups, or as a whole class.

Encourage students to use pantomime, simple costumes and props, or puppet shows to "pull it all together" as they imagine themselves in the following scenarios.

1. Water, Water Everywhere and Not a Drop to Drink!
Imagine that you are stranded on a desert island. The sun is beating down on you; your throat is as dry as the sand burning the soles of your feet. You drag yourself across miles and miles of desert until you finally come to the ocean. Pantomime this experience.

2. Dress for Success!
Put on an imaginary coat, scarf, boots, gloves, and hat. Go out an imaginary door, return to the same room, and remove all the clothing.

3. You're Late, You're Late, for a Very Important Date!
Imagine that you're late for school. Show your panic by quickly getting dressed, eating a fast breakfast, grabbing your books, and dashing out the door.

4. But No Elephants!
Imagine that you've found a stray pet—any kind of pet you want. Your parents say you can't keep it. Try to convince them to allow you to make this pet part of your family.

5. Lost and Found!
Pretend that you are allowed to keep the pet . . . but it runs away. Role-play or pantomime how you would report your missing pet to the police.

Build a Tale

Young children delight in fairy tales, folktales, and legends—and with good reasons! In addition to spanning cultures and providing hours of entertainment, these archetypal stories tap many critical-thinking skills. Guide children to use the critical-thinking skill of synthesis to build a class fairy tale. Here's how:

Materials for each group:
- slips of paper
- pencils
- hat, bag, bowl, or other container

Directions:

1. Arrange children in groups of five or six.

2. Explain that each group will create a fairy tale.

3. Have each child write a common noun on a slip of paper. You may want to provide some sample nouns such as *balloon, apple, basket.*

4. Have a volunteer in each group collect the slips of paper and place them in a container.

5. Ask group members to form a circle and count off, each child taking a number.

6. Direct the first person in each group to select a slip of paper from the hat and use the word to make up the first sentence in the fairy tale. Of course, the sentence should begin with the phrase "Once upon a time . . ." Another student should record the sentence. (As a variation, groups can tape-record their stories.)

7. Have the second player in each group select another slip of paper, repeat the sentence the first player has said, and add a second sentence using the new word.

8. The story builds as each player takes a turn.

9. The last player reads the entire story to the class.

Games Galore

This activity helps children develop their synthesizing skills by challenging them to create an original game from an assortment of commonplace materials. Before class, fill seven or eight large envelopes with an assortment of the following materials:

- straws
- paper clips
- paper tubes

- gum balls
- index cards
- spools of thread

- rubber bands
- safety pins
- buttons

Vary the contents of each envelope slightly.

When class begins, assemble children into groups of three to five members and give each an envelope of materials. Explain that students are to use the materials to invent their own game. It may have a board, but it does not have to. Students do not have to use all the materials in the envelope, nor do they have to use them in their current form. The paper clip, for example, can be stretched out, and the paper tube can be cut or unwound. Students can use an index card to jot down the rules of their game. Give children ample time to invent their games.

Have each group share its game by showing how it is played.

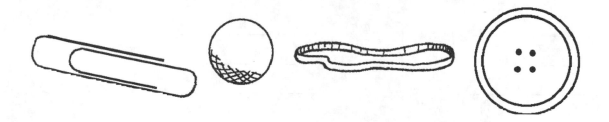

Name _____

Use It Well
· · · · · · · · · · · · · · ·

What is an egg carton for? It holds eggs, but you can use it for many other things, too.

Think of different ways to use each thing on this page.
Write down as many ideas as you can.

1. Egg carton

_____

_____

2. Newspaper

_____

_____

3. Clothespins

_____

_____

4. Plastic ring holders

_____

_____

5. Ball of string

_____

_____

_____

6. Bottle tops

_____

_____

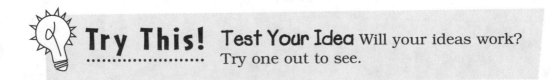

Try This! **Test Your Idea** Will your ideas work?
· · · · · · · · · Try one out to see.

Paint a Rainbow

You can mix red, blue, and yellow to make other colors. Mix paints to find out what colors you need to make purple, green, and orange. Then fill in the color chart. Use the colors you made to complete the rainbow.

COLOR CHART:

purple = _____ + _____

green   = _____ + _____

orange = _____ + _____

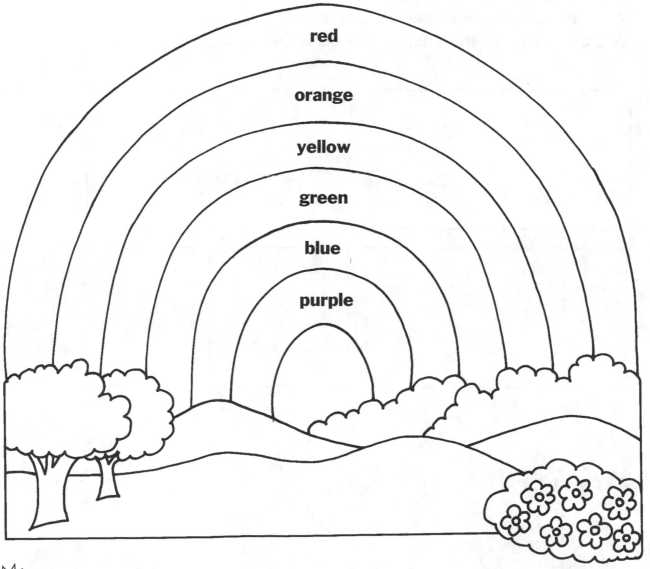

red

orange

yellow

green

blue

purple

 **Try This!** **Learn More** Read a book to find out more about rainbows.

Name _____

Shape Pictures

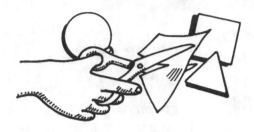 

Cut out these shapes.
Use them to make a figure or design.
You can use all the shapes or just some.
You can write on the shapes and color them, too.

Try This!

Name It Think of a title for the shape picture you made.

122

Fishy Stuff

This activity draws together the various critical-thinking skills children have learned thus far, focusing on synthesis. You can use this activity on its own or with a science lesson.

1. Start with a Story To begin, read children a story that involves characters that live in the water. For example, Syd Hoff's *Sammy the Seal* (HarperCollins) is a good choice for beginning learners. Explore how different animals need salt or fresh water to survive. Ask children which kind of water humans need.

2. Review Bodies of Water Ask children to recall some way that lakes are different from oceans. Write students' responses on the board, encouraging them to infer differences from the size and location of the oceans and lakes as well as the creatures that live in each. Remind students that rivers are made of fresh water—water without salt—and oceans are made of salt water. In addition, remind students that some creatures can live only in salt water; some creatures can live only in fresh water.

3. Hands on Experiment Explore the difference between fresh and salt water first-hand. You will need two small paper cups for each child, water, and some table salt.
- Have volunteers distribute two cups partly filled with water to each student. Ask children how they might learn more about the water they have. They might suggest tasting it, smelling it, touching it.
- Then ask students to add about a teaspoon of salt to one of their cups and to stir the water with a finger until the salt dissolves. Have students decide how the salty water is different from the fresh water. Does it taste different? Does it look or smell different?
- Lastly, ask students to discuss how they reached their conclusions. What thinking skills did they use?

4. Children as Authors Brainstorm a list of creatures that live in the ocean, such as whales, dolphins, lobsters, tuna, crabs, starfish, and seals. Then create a list of creatures that live in fresh water, such as salmon, turtles, frogs, and goldfish. Invite children to select one of these creatures as the subject for a story. When children have finished writing, have them copy their stories onto sheets of unlined paper folded down the middle and stapled in place. Suggest that children illustrate each page of the text and create a cover for their books. When the books are complete, display them on a shelf or table and allow students to peruse each other's writing at their leisure.

Story Time
·················

A story has three parts: a beginning, middle, and end. Use this page to help you think about the three parts of a story you will write.

Beginning
Who is in the story? Circle one character idea or write your own.

you   your friends   your family
superheroes   pets   _____

Where does the story take place? Circle one setting idea or write your own.

on earth   in outer space   in the park
at the beach   in the house   _____

When does the story take place? Circle one idea or write your own.

in the past   in the future   a summer day
winter day   a rainy day   _____

Middle
A story has a problem or goal that the main character has to solve or reach. Make notes about a problem your character might face.

_____

_____

_____

End
By the end of the story, the character works out the problem. Make notes about how your character might solve his or her problem.

_____

_____

_____

 **Try This!** **Draw** Draw a picture of your character in the
··················· setting of your story.

Answers

Recognizing and Recalling Activities

Place the Pictures, I (p. 14)
Beach: seashell, crab, sailboat, towel, fish

Supermarket: shopping cart, magazine, bread, bananas, milk

Place the Pictures II (p. 15)
Zoo: tree, monkey, elephant, tiger, bear

School: water fountain, telephone, crayons, computer, books, flag

A Is for . . . (p. 18)
Possible responses:

A is for apple	M is for mint
B is for banana	N is for nectarine
C is for carrot	O is for onion
D is for dandelion	P is for peach
E is for eggplant	Q is for quince
F is for flower	R is for raspberry
G is for grape	S is for strawberry
H is for hay or horse	T is for tomato
I is for iris	U is for uncle
J is for juniper	V is for vanilla
K is for kiwi	W is for watermelon
or kangaroo	Y is for yam
L is for lettuce	Z is for zebra

Who Lives Here? (p. 19)
Possible responses:
barn/cow; hive/bee; lake/fish; nest/bird; tree/squirrel; cave/bear;

Fruit Salad Chart (p. 20)

Fruits	red	yellow	purple	orange	round
1. orange	O	O	O	X	X
2. banana	O	X	O	O	O
3. lemon	O	X	O	O	O
4. grapes	O	O	X	O	X
5. pineapple	O	X	O	O	O

Word Meaning Fun (p. 21)
1. face, hands 2. eye, skin 3. teeth 4. heel, toe 5. ear 6. teeth 7. elbows 8. neck 9. body 10. eye

Distinguishing and Visualizing Activities

Where Do You Wear It? (p. 24)
1. hands 2. feet 3. body 4. feet 5. body 6. hands 7. feet 8. hands 9. body 10. body 11. head 12. head

Some Are the Same (p. 29)
Students should circle: 1. cow with bell 2. chicken with big tail 3. pony with no mane 4. puppy with bent ear 5. rabbit with no tail

Words and Pictures (p. 30)
1. This is something you eat. 2. This is something to wear on your head. 3. This is something you sleep on. 4. This is something you play with.

Fun with Words (p. 32)
The words can be written in any way that shows their meaning.
For example, *tall* can be written like this:

Naming Sets (p. 34)
1. Each has a stripe. 2. Each has 3 eyes. 3. Each has a tail. 4. Each has 6 legs.

Definitions and Examples (p. 36)
1. duck 2. stool 3. crayon 4. lettuce 5. book 6. clock

Mixed-Up Words (p. 37)
1. cup 2. glass 3. fork 4. sink 5. jar 6. dish 7. pot 8. spoon

Syllable Count (p. 38–39)

1 Syllable	*2 Syllables*	*3 Syllables*
bed	after	animal
cat	any	beautiful
day	bedtime	Dakota
eat	butter	dangerous
foot	circus	grasshopper
grass	letter	lumberyard
room	sunshine	Tennessee
sun	winter	united

Activities for Following Directions and Classifying Information

A Sorting Game (p. 42)
1. P 2. M 3. P 4. B 5. B 6. B
7. M 8. M 9. P 10. P 11. M 12. B

Does It Belong? (p. 43)
1. banana, apple, lemon, peach 2. doll, ball, yo-yo, top
3. lion, bull, monkey 4. hammer, wrench, saw, drill 5.
box, can, bag, basket 6. dress, skirt, sock, hat, robe 7.
football, soccer, baseball, tennis, skiing 8. beef, pork,
ham, hot dog

Letter Code (p. 44)
A fresh vegetable

Which Book? (p. 45)
sandwich-2; computer-3; cheese-2; cat-1; parrot-1;
vacuum-3; apple-2; dog-1; toaster-3

Making Groups (p. 46)
1. toy 2. letter 3. flower 4. hat 5. bed 6. number 7. bird
8. building

Walk This Way (p. 47)
Possible response: She stopped at the park. I know
because she walked six blocks, so she had to go past
the park. The other way is five blocks. The park is
halfway between her house and the library.

A Town Map (p. 48)
Maps will vary.

Color by Code (p. 50)

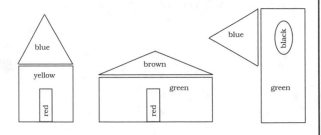

What Is What? (p. 51)
box 1: The car and boat are vehicles.
box 2: The first and last creatures are zorks.
box 3: The first and second shapes are tombats.
box 4: The first figure is a lork.

Riddle Me This (p. 52)
1. smile

    1. **s**ad
    2. lu**m**p
    3. f**i**ve
    4. co**l**d
    5. ston**e**

2. ten pigs
    1. s**t**op
    2. blu**e**
    3. bar**n**
    4. a**p**e
    5. t**i**ny
    6. **g**irl
    7. **s**ummer

Sequencing and Predicting Activities

Make a Puppet (p. 56)
a. 4 b. 1 c. 2 d. 3

End the Story (p. 57)
1. boy walking dog
2. girl feeding rabbit
3. fish in bowl

1,2,3 (p. 60)
3. Jess went to school.
1. Jess woke up.
2. Jess got dressed.

3. Kim rode down the street.
2. Kim put on her helmet.
1. Kim got on her bike.
or
3. Kim rode down the street.
1. Kim put on her helmet.
2. Kim got on her bike.

1. I get the bread.
3. I eat lunch.
2. I put on the jam.

Build a Castle (p. 61)
21 blocks are needed—one row of 6, one of 7, and one of 8. There are 36 blocks in the castle.

Words in Order (p. 62)
ant, bug, cab, dog, egg, fish, goat, hen, ice, jet, key, lid, man, nut, on, pan, queen, rat, sun, tub

As Easy as ABC (p. 63)
1. ape 2. hat 3. cow 4. apple 5. lock 6. cat
1. ape 2. bird 3. dish 4. hat 5. lid 6. man 7. pan 8. teeth

It's About Time (p. 64)
1. Day 3   2. Day 4   3. Day 1
4. Day 6   5. 7 days old

Busy Day (p. 65)
Possible response:

Buy bread and eggs	5
Pick up cleaning	4
Drop off cake at school bake sale	6
Mail letters and buy stamps	8
Return Mr. Robert's wrench	3
Buy food for Sally's frog	2
Leave shoes to be fixed	1
Eat lunch at the diner	7

What Will Happen? (p. 66)
get soft: soap, paper, sponge, dress, muffin, noodles; stay the same: fork, pail
melt: candle, ice cream, crayons, snowman, butter; stay the same: wagon, shoe, spoon

And Then . . . (p. 67)
1. c 2. b 3. a 4. c

Most Likely (p. 68)
1. hot 2. disappointed 3. school 4. admire it 5. excited 6. improve 7. a bigger size 8. full

Activities for Inferring and Drawing Conclusions

The Right Home (p. 72)
fish in bowl, dog in house, lion in den, bird in cage

What Is It? (p. 76)
1. tiger 2. sunflower 3. seal 4. moon 5. tree 6. bee 7. squirrel 8. cloud

What Can You Do? (p. 77)
Students should underline: 2, 3, 5, 6, 7

Clues for Conclusions (p. 79)
1. Jack was on his bike.
2. Lisa and Kim are in school.
3. Sam is making a sandwich.

Learning About the Vonce (p. 80)
Possible responses:
1. Yes, because the Vonce has a fur coat.
2. Yes, because it has webbed back feet.
3. Yes, because it has claws on its front feet.
4. Yes, because it has big, round ears.
5. No, because its front legs are short and have sharp claws. The claws might get caught in the ground.

Snap-Together Words (p. 81)
Possible responses:
1. backyard	yard in the back
2. teacup	cup for tea
3. billfold	place for bills; wallet
4. barnyard	yard near a barn
5. airline	airplane company
6. tiptoe	walk on toes
7. raindrop	drop of rain
8. sunrise	sun coming up; dawn
9. campground	grounds of a camp
10. masterpiece	best work

Crack the Code (p. 83)
1. 0 = B   1 = E   2 = A   3 = R
The word is BEAR.
2. 0 = B   1 = I   2 = R   3 = D
The word is BIRD.
3. 0 = D   1 = I   2 = M   3 = E
The word is DIME.

Evaluating Activities

Be an Editor (p. 87)
1. His belt is brown. 2. We have bunk beds. 3. Her cookies are great. 4. The beavers made it.

Pet Shopping (p. 89)
Possible responses:
cat—soft and warm / has mind of its own;
ant—works hard / not friendly;
parrot—sings sweetly / not cuddly;
elephant—smart / too big;
snake—interesting / hard to hold

Will It Fit? (p. 91)
1. magazine, letter, newspaper 2. thermos, sandwich, apple 3. paper clip, crayon, coins

Pick a Winner (p. 94)
Possible responses:
1. bird   6. ground
2. coat   7. ocean
3. plane   8. sun
4. ice   9. banana
5. worm   10. pillow

Analyzing Activities

Finish the Picture (p. 100)
Students should draw: 1. leg 2. wheel 3. ear 4. petal 5. door 6. step 7. arm 8. claw

What Is Missing? (p. 101)
1. hand 2. ear 3. wing 4. wheel 5. handle 6. lace

Real or Make-Believe? (p. 106)
1. No 2. Yes 3. No 4. Yes 5. Yes 6. No 7. No 8. Yes 9. No 10. Yes

Alike and Different (p. 107)
Possible response:

bicycle		**rocket**
Different	Same	Different
slow	Vehicles	fast
2 wheels	Made of Metal	no wheels
land		air
1 person		more than 1 person
small		big

Does It Rhyme? (p. 108)
Yes; No; No; Yes; Yes; No; Yes; Yes; No; No
HEARS A YOLK

Double Fun (p. 110)
1. timepiece
2. look at
3. stick
4. small animal
5. goes away
6. part of a tree
7. show where something is
8. things counted in a game

What's the Meaning? (p. 111)
Students should color: 1. girl laughing 2. man at desk

Ha! Ha! (p. 112)
1. b 2. a 3. d 4. c
Try This! Possible answers:
1. Because they don't know the words
2. A spelling bee

Synthesizing Activities

Paint a Rainbow (p. 121)
purple = red + blue;
green = blue + yellow;
orange = red + yellow